“Marla’s step-by-step program will give you a tremendous edge in being chosen as a contestant—not to mention helping you to develop the proper strategy and positive attitude it takes to be a winner!”

David Greenfield, producer of “Battlestars,” “All Star Blitz,” and “The Dating Game”

“Marla Schram Schwartz has captured every nuance of being on a game show. Her book will make my job easier because it answers all the questions people have about becoming a contestant.”

Beverly Pomerantz, contestant coordinator of “One Million Dollar Chance of a Lifetime”

“Because of the knowledge and confidence Marla’s program gave me, I was chosen as a contestant and won over $25,000!”

Larry Goss, winner on “All Star Blitz”

Be a TV GAME SHOW *Winner!*

MARLA SCHRAM SCHWARTZ

Foreword by

MONTY HALL

HARMONY BOOKS
New York

Published by Harmony Books, a division of Crown Publishers, Inc., 225 Park Avenue South, New York, New York 10003 and represented in Canada by the Canadian MANDA Group

HARMONY and colophon are trademarks of Crown Publishers, Inc.

Manufactured in the United States of America

Design by Claudia DePolo

Library of Congress Cataloging-in-Publication Data

Schwartz, Marla Schram.
Be a TV game show winner!

1. Game shows. I. Title.
PN1992.8.Q5S39 1988 791.45'5 87-21229
ISBN 0-517-56775-X (pbk.)

10 9 8 7 6 5 4 3 2 1

First Edition

Contents

Foreword

by Monty Hall

Although millions of words have been written about game shows, no one has researched the subject as thoroughly as Marla Schram Schwartz. Everything about game shows is covered in this book—from facts about the shows to tips for people hoping to get on them.

What isn't covered by Marla are the thousands of hours of frustration spent in a production office trying to come up with an idea that hasn't been used before. For after forty-plus years of game shows, every permutation and combination has made its way over a producer's desk.

My dentist sent me a game show genius some years back. He opened up his portfolio and started to describe his new show:

''You have these four celebrities who serve as your panel and an emcee who brings out various people who have odd occupations. The panel's job is to identify that occupation.''

I sat there and stared at him for a while, not believing my ears. Finally I said, ''Haven't you ever heard of 'What's My Line?'? Mark Goodson will be astonished to learn that you've just invented a show that's been on the air for nineteen years!''

Almost every week I have to tell some friend of a friend that his idea (a) has been used before, (b) is on the air now, or (c) is something close to what we have been working on. (That's why we do not accept submissions from the outside.)

We have many stories about what people will do to get on a show, because of the unusual way in which they were selected for ''Let's Make a Deal.'' Everyone gathered in lines in front of the studio, and from that gathering thirty-six people were chosen to sit on the trading floor. Most of them came in costumes. Their own idea, by the way! (This was not a feature in the early shows and evolved from the prospective contestants themselves.) It was always quite a colorful scene.

When the selection process started, the frenzy grew. The people making the selection tried to give us a cross-section of young and old, fat and thin, black, yellow, white, whatever. Moving up and down the line making the selections was a hazardous job. Some people felt that the more extroverted they were in the line-up, the better their chances were, that wasn't true. Our selection people could easily see through artificial exuberance, and many people who were standing on their heads were astounded to find that they were passed by.

One of my favorite facts about ''Let's Make a Deal'' was that in 4,300 broadcasts with approximately 45,000 contestants, I had only one lady who became visibly upset when she was passed by (she hit me over the head with a little stuffed tiger). Then during a break, she asked to have the microphone when the taping was over, so she could apologize. She said, ''I don't know what came over me. I am a lawyer and I am supposed to be able to contain my emotions. But when Monty walked off, I got carried away. I apologize to Monty, I apologize to the audience and to all those contestants over the years whom I thought were 'crazy' for jumping up and down when they were chosen.''

Here are a few other memorable deals:

We opened up the curtain one time to reveal our model, Carol Merrill, standing with a tether rope. But, at the first sound of the door opening, the baby elephant that was supposed to have been the prize trumpeted his farewell and bolted from the stage, and the studio, and was last seen gallumphing down Prospect Avenue.

Another time, I asked a woman if she would trade the curtain for what was inside a box of fried chicken. She agreed. I lifted the box lid, and there was a beautiful watch case, and inside the beautiful watch case . . . nothing! The $2,500 watch had been lifted backstage between the rehearsal and the show. Things got a bit hysterical for a few minutes as Jay started tossing out pieces of chicken, looking for the watch. We made up a cover story, saying that the watch had been locked in the safe and no one could find the person with the combination. (Of course, the lady received a duplicate watch.)

Then, I once offered a man wearing a scuba mask and flippers $500 if he could produce a ''pool ball.'' Using his noodle and remembering a previous deal behind a door, he ran across the set, flippers flapping, and removed the eight ball from a pool table prize, flipped back triumphantly, and collected his $500.

Everyone who is in the game show business has hundreds of stories to tell. Basically, all you need to know is in this book. But if you want to hear more—call me someday. You won't believe what I have to tell you! But you *can* believe what's in this book.

Acknowledgments

I could not have written this book without the cooperation and support of the many people involved in the game show industry. Therefore, let me first thank all the contestant coordinators who took the time to answer my many questions about their shows: Donna Jean Steines, Jerry Modine, Ingrid Woodson, Lisa Furubotten, Andrea Carroll, Beth Fiance, Joyce Weiss Stevens, Tony Pandolfo, Peggy Lavell, Jeff Sharping, Ida Mae McKinzie, and Stephanie Hope.

I also want to thank all the contestants who were so kind to share their game show experiences with me: Cheryl Reinwand, Angela Grace and Mark Fogarty, Lisa and Dan Smith, Connie and Steve Rutenbar, Steve Ray, Barbara Schnell, Stacey Brower, Tammie Eisele, Martin Gold, Christy Nemetz, Will and Sue Dent, Sue and Mike Hensley, David and Lisa Mills, Will and Lauri Johnson, Cary and Cathy Schorr, Thom McKee, Ellen Glasgow, Dinah and Larry Goss, Lori and Michael McCabe, and Rhoda Stone.

Many thanks to producers Mark Goodson, Bob Synes, Rick Rosner, Phillip and Frank Wayne, Bob Stewart, George Vosburgh, Bob Noah, Burt Wheeler, Gary Johnson, Joe Neustein, Dan Enright, Art Alisi, Merrill Heatter, Ron Greenberg, Jay Wolpert, and Merv Griffin for their valuable time, photo permissions, and helpful insights into the game show industry.

I am also grateful to the hosts who granted me interviews and/or use of their photographs: Monty Hall, Bob Barker, Jim Lange, John Davidson, and Dick Clark.

A big thank you for photo permissions goes to Mark Ragonese, Orion TV Productions, Century Towers Productions, Twentieth

Century-Fox, Aaron Perry, Goodson-Todman, Leo Ziffren, hostesses Vanna White and Karen Thomas, Brian Mitchell, and the many other celebrities who appear in the book.

I am very grateful to Leo Howard of Howard and Howard, an accounting firm in Encino, California, for sharing with me his knowledge and expertise on the tax laws for winning cash and prizes on a game show.

To a man who's hard to locate, producer Norman Blumenthal, for use of his "Recipe for a Successful Game Show."

A very sincere thanks to popular game show host Monty Hall for graciously taking the time out of his busy schedule to write the foreword to my book. Everyone told me he was one of the most well-liked hosts in the game show industry, and I certainly understand why!

A million thanks to Mr. Game Show himself—Fred Wostbrook—for his fantastic photos, interesting trivia and history, great connections, and continued encouragement with this projetc. I don't think there is anyone in this world who knows more about game shows than Fred, and he is very generous with his knowledge.

A special "thank you" to my talented literary agent, Meredith Bernstein, for her hard work and solid belief in my book idea.

I am especially thankful to Melissa Schwarz, my wonderful editor at Harmony Books, for her valuable suggestions and assistance with this project. Her enthusiasm and kindness made my job as a writer much more enjoyable!

My biggest thanks without a doubt goes to good friend and contestant coordinator Beverly Pomerantz. She turned me on to countless contestants, producers, hosts, and other game show people who contributed heavily to *Be a TV Game Show Winner!* Besides her wonderful help and fantastic connections, she has given me something really special—her loyal friendship! Bev, I am gratefully indebted to you!

Last, but certainly not least, my heartfelt thanks to Maria Sanchez; my husband, Arnie; and all my family and friends for their support and encouragement. I love you!

Introduction

It's hard to believe that I still get goosebumps just by thinking about the TV games shows that I've played on, but it's true! I can close my eyes and instantly relive every exhilarating moment.

"ALL STAR BLITZ" HOST PETER MARSHALL: "For $5,000 and the game, Marla, what is the correct phrase?"

ME: "Nothing ventured, nothing gained."

PETER MARSHALL: "Congratulations! You've just won $5,000!" (Lights flash!)

"CHILD'S PLAY" HOST BILL CULLEN: "Marla, for a total of $7,500, what word are we looking for?"

ME: "Proud!"

BILL CULLEN: "That's it! You're a winner!" (Bells ring!)

"MATCH GAME" HOST GENE RAYBURN: "You've won $2,000 on your last two games. If you match answers with the celebrity player of your choice, you'll win the $5,000 bonus, making your total earnings $7,000. Ready? 'Incredible blank.' "

ME: "Hulk."

GENE RAYBURN: "You did it! You've just won the $5,000 bonus! You're now a three-time winner and our returning champion!" (Buzzers sound!)

My game show experiences remain the most exciting in my life. The "rush" of winning was absolutely overwhelming. I felt like I had just won a gold medal at the Olympics and millions of people were witness to the fact that I was a champion!

When people discover that I have been a game show contestant, they bombard me with all kinds of questions like, "What shows were you on?" "How much did you win?" "Did you get to keep the prizes?" "Did you have to take a written test first?" And, of course, "How can *I* get on a game show?" Why does their curiosity become almost obsessive? Because the reality has set in—if I can be on a game show and win, then they can too.

If you have ever found yourself in front of your television set watching a game show and muttering, "Oh, I know the answer to that question," this book is for you. It's frustrating to give correct answers that would have earned you a car, a boat, a vacation, or thousands of dollars if only you had been playing the game in the studio rather than in your own living room. People from all walks of life share similar fantasies of being discovered by a talent scout or becoming filthy rich overnight—and where else but on a game show can you be seen by millions of people and earn thousands of dollars with absolutely no experience?

Are the people who are accepted as contestants any better or smarter players than those who aren't? Smarter, no; better, yes. You don't have to be a genius to be on a game show, but you do have to know the ins and outs. You must understand what the producers and coordinators are looking for, and you must stand out in that "would-be contestant" crowd.

My game show triumphs were not accidents; nor were they just a matter of luck. On each show I tried out for, I studied the contestants' behavior. I worked hard developing various game strategies, making sure to practice them thoroughly before my taping day arrived. Later, I even took a job as a writer on a game show. I wanted to learn everything I could about how they operate. After winning on "Match Game," "All Star Blitz," and "Child's Play," I knew that all my research had paid off. Thanks to my many victories I have become known as the perfect contestant type, which has led to my being invited to film many pilot game shows as well.

From my experiences and research, I developed a formula for being chosen and winning. Implementing these special strategies and techniques, I soon discovered that with each new game show challenge, I became stronger and more capable of controlling my fears and insecurities. I can honestly say that the knowledge and confidence I gained was even more valuable to me than my prizes and being famous.

Bob Stewart, producer of "$100,000 Pyramid," "Chain Reaction," and "Double Talk," sums it up quite nicely: "Just being chosen makes you special. You're on TV, you can VCR yourself, and it's definitely something to tell your grandkids!"

Production companies desperately need good players. Unfortunately, the majority of people who interview for game shows don't "cut it" for one reason or another. That is why producers will sometimes interview hundreds of people at once and may accept only one out of every eighty people they interview. Then that one person will be put into a file and still may never appear on the show.

Why is it that only a small percentage of those who interview actually become contestants? Fred Wostbrock, contestant coordinator for "Battlestars," "Crosswits," and "Your Number's Up," explains, "The odds of getting on a game show are tough because it takes advance preparation. The trouble is people don't know how to prepare for their interview or taping because they don't know what to expect."

Be a TV Game Show Winner! will help you decide which shows to try out for and then guide you through each step along the way. It also lists the important interview requirements for the top ten game shows on television and teaches the inside secrets for looking and acting like an appealing game show contestant. With this book you will be totally prepared for your taping day with tips on what to expect at the studio, what kind of clothing to bring, how to calm your nerves, and what you should and should not do while backstage or on camera. Getting ready to appear on TV is similar to rehearsing for a graduation or wedding. All you need are instructions on where to walk and how to act to ensure that things run smoothly. Special occasions demand special attention, and game shows are *very special!*

In chapters 4 and 5 you will learn how to increase your

chances of winning with helpful visualization techniques, positive-mental-attitude exercises, and special playing strategies for every current game show. To help sharpen your game-playing skills, easy, moderately difficult, and hard puzzles and trivia questions are provided as well. There is advice on how best to handle the IRS and your cash and prize winnings, in addition to information on how game shows are created, sold, and produced.

Be a TV Game Show Winner! will not guarantee that you will be chosen as a television game show contestant. Nor will it guarantee that you will win a truckload of cash and prizes. What it *will* do is put you ahead of the vast majority of people with whom you will interview and compete. And if you are chosen as a contestant and lose, chances are you will know exactly where you went wrong so that you can turn around and try again.

Regardless of the outcome as a contestant, you will always be a winner because all shows award consolation prizes worth up to $1,000. If you figure your time on a per-hour basis, even a loss is a win! Also, think of the courage it took to appear in front of millions of people on national TV. You will have made new friends at the studio and had fun along the way. Your family and friends will be proud of you. The world will somehow know you a little better. And you'll come home with an experience that you will cherish forever.

But let's face it, you can't win a state lottery unless you buy a ticket. The same is true of game shows. No one is going to hand you large amounts of cash and prizes on a silver platter while you're sitting at home in your easy chair. You must take the first step!

On every game show, every day, someone walks away a winner. If you're tired of being a spectator and want to become a participant in this great American phenomenon, all you have to do to make your dream a reality is prepare yourself. So sit back and enjoy my book—it's sure to change your life.

Chapter 1

Tactics: Where to Begin

There are more than twenty different game, talent, and romance shows on network and syndicated television and a lot more on various cable stations. This large selection means you can try out for only those games that will give you the best chance of winning.

To begin, review the current game shows in your local *TV Guide* and make a preliminary list. Most of the game and talent programs throughout the country air from 9:00 A.M. to 12:00 noon, and 3:30 P.M. to 9:00 P.M., Monday through Friday, and 10:30 A.M. to 8:00 P.M. on Saturdays and Sundays.

Next, check the front of the *L.A. Times* Sunday classified section for announcements from game shows that are looking for contestants. (If you do not live in California, simply call the *L.A. Times* office to obtain a copy.) If producers are advertising in the paper or at the end of their game on television, you can be sure they need you and that your interview will be set up quickly.

You will be able to interview sooner for *new* game shows as

Ads for game show contestants from the *Los Angeles Times*

well, because it takes time for a new show to gain the popularity that later results in more people trying out. "Wheel of Fortune" and "The Price Is Right" are good examples of games that are popular now and have hundreds of people wanting to become contestants. Therefore, the probability of your receiving an interview for these shows in the near future is pretty slim.

Sometimes at the end of a show or in the Sunday classified section of the paper you will hear that the game's contestant coordinators are traveling to a certain city to recruit new players for regular or special weeks. If they will be near where you live, this could be a very convenient chance to interview. Many producers will fly you out to L.A. and pay for your accommodations if you are a contestant during a special week.

GAME SHOW FACTSHEETS

Once you have a list of game shows in mind that you especially like, put together a factsheet on each one so that you will be ready to select those that are best for you. Completed factsheets for the current top ten TV game shows are provided in this chapter. They include all the information you need to try out for the following shows:

"Card Sharks"
"Hollywood Squares"
"Jeopardy!"
"The New Newlywed Game"
"The Price Is Right"
"$25,000 Pyramid" and "$100,000 Pyramid"
"Sale of the Century"
"Scrabble"
"Super Password"
"Wheel of Fortune"

If you are interested in interviewing for a game show that is not listed, you can do your own research and collect the appropriate information on a blank factsheet like the one provided.

To complete your own factsheet, write in the name of the show you are considering and its host. You will find the names of the executive producer, production company, and producer at the end of the show's credits, and you can obtain their telephone numbers from directory assistance.

Another way to obtain the phone number of a current

game show or production company is to call the general station number (e.g., Channel 7, KABC). The station, in turn, will give you the number of the show. You will receive the contestant coordinator's name and phone number when you call the production company.

You can obtain the interview date, time, address, and requirements from the contestant coordinator when you call for an appointment. The taping date, time, and address will be supplied by the coordinator after you have passed the interview.

Some shows air in the evening, as well as during the day. If there is a nighttime version of the show, be sure to let the contestant coordinator know that it is your first choice. Producers usually offer larger amounts of cash and more exciting prizes at night to capitalize on the larger viewing audience.

Next, fill in the number of contestants that compete on the show and list any people who will be playing with you (e.g., spouse, family, celebrities).

Under "Necessary Playing Skills" describe the type of game show and the major skills required to play it. These points will be explained in detail in chapter 2.

Briefly describe how to play and win the game under the heading "Object of Game." After watching the show on TV a few times, you will have a solid understanding of how it is played, but don't worry, the *exact* rules—of both the main game and the bonus round—will be explained to you at your interview.

You can fill in what type of prizes are offered just from watching the show on TV. To find out what the *top* prizes are, ask the coordinator when you set up your interview appointment.

Use "Comments" for any miscellaneous information such as contestant searches, special weeks, dress code, typical behavior you observe on the show, and so on.

At the bottom of the factsheet, check off how well you play the game. Watch and play along with the contestants at least twice before rating your playing ability. Try to be as objective as possible. If you're watching the show at home and can't think of the answers in the time allotted, you'll never guess them while playing on TV. Don't give yourself excuses like, "Oh, I was just about to say that." If you're honest with yourself about your abilities, you should have a good chance of getting on a show and winning.

TV GAME SHOW FACTSHEET

GAME SHOW: ______________________

HOST: ______________________

EXECUTIVE PRODUCER/PRODUCTION COMPANY: ______________________

PRODUCER: ______________________

CONTESTANT COORDINATOR: ______________________

PHONE NUMBER: ______________________

INTERVIEW ADDRESS: ______________________

INTERVIEW DATE AND TIME: ______________________

INTERVIEW REQUIREMENTS: ______________________

TAPING STUDIO ADDRESS: ______________________

TAPING DAYS AND HOURS: ______________________

NUMBER OF CONTESTANTS COMPETING/PLAYING: ______________________

NECESSARY PLAYING SKILLS: ______________________

OBJECT OF GAME: ______________________

PRIZES AVAILABLE: ______________________

COMMENTS: ______________________

I PLAY THIS GAME: [ ] Very well [ ] Well [ ] Okay
[ ] Poorly

Card Sharks

HOST: (Daytime) Bob Eubanks; (Nighttime) Bill Rafferty

EXECUTIVE PRODUCER: Mark Goodson

PRODUCER: Mimi O'Brien

CONTESTANT COORDINATOR: Donna Jean Steines and Beverly Morrison

PHONE NUMBER: (213) 520-1234

INTERVIEW ADDRESS: 6430 Sunset Boulevard, 14th floor, Hollywood, California 90028

INTERVIEW DATE AND TIME: Two to four interviews a day, five to six days a week.

INTERVIEW REQUIREMENTS: You will be asked to stand up and introduce yourself. Then you will take a written test with questions similar to those on the show. If you are asked to stay, you will play a mock game in front of the producer. If the producer is not available, you will be asked to return for a second interview.

TAPING STUDIO ADDRESS: CBS Television City, 7800 Beverly Boulevard, Los Angeles, California 90028

TAPING DAYS AND HOURS: Varies

NUMBER OF CONTESTANTS COMPETING/PLAYING: Two contestants compete against each other.

NECESSARY PLAYING SKILLS: Requires logic when answering questions and when guessing whether the next card will be higher or lower.

OBJECT OF GAME: You must guess how many people will answer a question a certain way, thereby obtaining control of the cards. You must then guess if the next card will be higher or lower. When you have correctly revealed all your playing cards, you will win the game. Best two games out of three wins the match.

PRIZES AVAILABLE: (Daytime) Combined total of $100,000 in cash and cars; (Nighttime) Combined total of $75,000 in cash and prizes.

COMMENTS: Be outgoing and opinionated. Briefly explain why you are choosing that number of people or why you are guessing higher or lower. Special weeks for kids and teens. Contestant searches throughout the U.S.

I PLAY THIS GAME: [ ] Very well [ ] Well [ ] Okay [ ] Poorly

THE NEW NEWLYWED GAME

HOST: Bob Eubanks

PRODUCTION COMPANY: Barris Productions

EXECUTIVE PRODUCER: Jeff Wald

PRODUCER: Scott Sternberg

CONTESTANT SUPERVISOR: Jeffrey B. Scharping

PHONE NUMBER: (213) 469-4907

INTERVIEW ADDRESS: Sunset-Gower Studios, 1420 North Beachwood Drive, Stage 7, Hollywood, California 90028

INTERVIEW DATE AND TIME: Varies

INTERVIEW REQUIREMENTS: You will be asked to fill out a short questionnaire, then to play a mock game lasting up to twenty minutes in front of the coordinator and/or producer. Sometimes a second interview observed by the producer is required.

TAPING STUDIO ADDRESS: Sunset-Gower Studios, 1420 North Beachwood Drive, Stage 7, Hollywood, California 90028

TAPING DAYS AND HOURS: Varies

NUMBER OF CONTESTANTS COMPETING/PLAYING: Four newly-married couples compete against each other.

NECESSARY PLAYING SKILLS: Being able to predict what your spouse will say.

OBJECT OF GAME: Husbands and wives try to match each other's answers to gain points and win the game.

PRIZES AVAILABLE: Prizes of your choice including: appliances, trips, cars, etc.

COMMENTS: You will be asked to produce a marriage certificate proving that you have been married two years or less. You and your spouse must be vocal and maintain a high level of excitement. The producers are looking for outgoing couples who have a great sense of fun. Special weeks for alumni, seniors, others.

I PLAY THIS GAME: [ ] Very well [ ] Well [ ] Okay [ ] Poorly

HOLLYWOOD SQUARES

HOST: John Davidson

EXECUTIVE PRODUCER: Rick Rosner

PRODUCER: Ernie Dimassa

CONTESTANT COORDINATOR: Stephenie Hope

INTERVIEW PHONE NUMBER: (213) 444-7455

INTERVIEW ADDRESS: NBC Studios, 3000 Alameda Boulevard, Burbank, California 91523

INTERVIEW DATE AND TIME: Held at the same time as the taping date and time.

INTERVIEW REQUIREMENTS: The contestant coordinator interviews fifty to one hundred people from the audience, after the show's taping. She will ask you a few questions to determine if you have the outgoing personality required to play. The coordinator might need to interview you a second time, which she would then do over the telephone.

TAPING STUDIO ADDRESS: NBC Studios, 3000 Alameda Boulevard, Burbank, California 91523

TAPING DAYS AND HOURS: Sundays and Mondays every other week, 2:30 P.M. to 9:30 P.M.

NUMBER OF CONTESTANTS COMPETING/PLAYING: Two contestants play against each other.

NECESSARY PLAYING SKILLS: Logic and luck combined with light general knowledge and knowledge of trivia.

OBJECT OF GAME: You must agree or disagree with a panel of

nine celebrities' answers to earn three Xs or Os in a row, either diagonally, horizontally, or vertically. If you win two out of three matches, you win the game.

PRIZES AVAILABLE: Cars (valued up to $30,000), trips (international and local), cash (up to $3,000 for playing on five shows).

COMMENTS: They are looking for energetic, friendly players.

I PLAY THIS GAME: [ ] Very well [ ] Well [ ] Okay [ ] Poorly

JEOPARDY!

HOST: Alex Trebek

PRODUCTION COMPANY: Merv Griffin Enterprises

PRODUCER: Alex Trebek

ASSOCIATE PRODUCERS: Jules Minton, Sherry Hilber

CONTESTANT COORDINATORS: Greg Muntean, Ingrid Woodson, and Glenn Kagan

PHONE NUMBER: (213) 466-3931

INTERVIEW ADDRESS: 5800 Sunset Boulevard, Building 11, Hollywood, California 90028

INTERVIEW DATE AND TIME: Mondays, Thursdays, and Fridays, 10:30 A.M. or 1:30 P.M.

INTERVIEW REQUIREMENTS: Only one interview is required, and it could last up to 1½ hours. You will be given a fifty-question general-knowledge written test. Then you will play a mock game in front of two contestant coordinators.

TAPING STUDIO ADDRESS: 5800 Sunset Boulevard, Stage 1, Hollywood, California 90028

TAPING DAYS AND HOURS: Tuesdays and Wednesdays, 2:30 P.M. to 8 P.M., five shows a day, ten shows a week.

NUMBER OF CONTESTANTS COMPETING/PLAYING: Three contestants compete against each other.

NECESSARY PLAYING SKILLS: A quick recall of a vast amount of obscure trivia.

OBJECT OF GAME: You must answer as many questions as possible in six subject categories so that you will have the largest amount of earnings at the end of the game.

PRIZES AVAILABLE: $75,000 in cash and trips.

COMMENTS: They are looking for intelligent, self-confident, and friendly players. Special weeks for seniors, teens, tournament of champions. Your travel expenses will be paid for if you are appearing on a "special week." Contestant searches throughout the U. S.

I PLAY THIS GAME: [ ] Very well [ ] Well [ ] Okay [ ] Poorly

The Price Is Right

HOST: Bob Barker

EXECUTIVE PRODUCER: Frank Wayne

PRODUCERS: Phillip Wayne and Roger Dobkowitz

CONTESTANTS CHOSEN BY: Producer, Phillip Wayne

PHONE NUMBER: (213) 852-2624

TAPING/INTERVIEWING ADDRESS: CBS Television City, 7800 Beverly Boulevard, Studio 33, Hollywood, California 90036

TAPING DAYS AND HOURS: Shows are taped on Mondays, Tuesdays, and Wednesdays, two shows a day, each show one-hour long. You should arrive at 7:30 A.M. for the 2:15 P.M. show and at 11:30 A.M. for the 6:15 P.M. show.

INTERVIEW REQUIREMENTS: In order to become a contestant, you must first write for studio-audience tickets to The Price Is Right, 7800 Beverly Boulevard, Los Angeles, California 90036. It will take approximately two to eight months to receive them, unless you ask for specific dates. Once in line to see the show, you will be given a name tag and number. The producer, Phillip Wayne, will talk to four or five people at a time, asking them very brief questions to get their immediate reactions, until he has interviewed the entire audience. If he wants to use you as a contestant, he will secretly cue one of his assistants, who will write down your name and number. He will then look over his "cue list" to see who has the most energy and the most natural feeling for the show. If you are selected as a contestant, you will be asked, sometime during the taping, to "come on down!"

NUMBER OF CONTESTANTS COMPETING/PLAYING: Nine contestants per show are selected to play individual games.

NECESSARY PLAYING SKILLS: Skilled at pricing merchandise.

OBJECT OF GAME: You must come closest to guessing the actual retail value of different types of merchandise to win those prizes. The winners go on to spin for the opportunity to guess the prices of the more valuable merchandise contained in the showcase.

PRIZES AVAILABLE: Cars, trips, and cash totaling up to $100,000.

COMMENTS: They are looking for warm, enthusiastic players with a "sparkle in their eyes."

I PLAY THIS GAME: [ ] Very well [ ] Well [ ] Okay [ ] Poorly

$25,000 PYRAMID (DAYTIME) AND $100,000 PYRAMID (NIGHTTIME)

HOST: Dick Clark

EXECUTIVE PRODUCER: Bob Stewart

SUPERVISING PRODUCER: Anne Marie Schmidt

PRODUCERS: David Michaels, Francine Bergman

CONTESTANT COORDINATOR: Lisa Furubotten

INTERVIEW PHONE NUMBER: (213) 461-3746

INTERVIEW ADDRESS: 1717 North Highland Avenue, Suite 605, Hollywood, California 90028

INTERVIEW DATE AND TIME: Mondays, Tuesdays, and Wednesdays, 11:00 A.M. or 1:00 P.M.

INTERVIEW REQUIREMENTS: Twenty-five to thirty people will receive a fifteen-minute briefing of the rules and various pointers.

Eight people at a time will play a mock game. Certain people will be eliminated, then you will play another mock game but with more difficult material. The first interview lasts about one hour. The second interview is scheduled within a month of the first unless you are from out of town, in which case they will schedule you sooner. You will play the small Pyramid and the big Pyramid game. If selected, you will be notified within one week, by letter, and then put into an active file, which is used for up to one year.

TAPING STUDIO ADDRESS: CBS Studios, 7800 Beverly Boulevard, Hollywood, California 90028

TAPING DAYS AND HOURS: Thursdays and Fridays, fifteen shows in two days.

NUMBER OF CONTESTANT COMPETING/PLAYING: Two teams (one contestant and one celebrity) compete against each other.

NECESSARY PLAYING SKILLS: Good vocabulary and skilled at quickly communicating synonyms and word clues.

OBJECT OF GAME: You and your partner take turns guessing the seven words from one of the categories that you have chosen to describe, by using word or phrase clues, within thirty seconds. Each team plays three rounds, switches celebrity partners, and then plays three more rounds. The team that guesses the most words goes on to play the big Pyramid.

PRIZES AVAILABLE: (Daytime) $100,000; (Nighttime) No limit on money, but you may only be on five shows.

COMMENTS: They are looking for energetic, enthusiastic, knowledgeable people. If you are put in the active file but are not selected to play, you may try out again in three months. This should give you more than enough time to practice your communication skills. Special weeks for teens, blind people (on "$25,000 Pyramid" only). A $100,000 tournament is held every six to ten weeks on "$100,000 Pyramid."

I PLAY THIS GAME: [ ] Very well [ ] Well [ ] Okay [ ] Poorly

SALE OF THE CENTURY

HOST: Jim Perry

PRODUCTION COMPANY: Reg Grundy

EXECUTIVE PRODUCER: Bob Noah

PRODUCER: Burt Wheeler

CONTESTANT COORDINATOR: Andrea Carroll

PHONE NUMBER: (213) 284-8644

INTERVIEW ADDRESS: 9911 West Pico Boulevard, Suite 720, Los Angeles, California 90035

INTERVIEW DATE AND TIME: Varies

INTERVIEW REQUIREMENTS: The first interview could last up to two hours. You will take a fifty-question general-knowledge written test. Then you will stand up before a group of anywhere from 75 to 200 people and say something about yourself. Your written and oral tests will be graded during a short break, and then the coordinator will make the first cut. If chosen, you will be asked to come back, usually within a week, with a couple of funny or unusual stories about yourself. The second interview will last about one hour, and you will be asked to expand on your stories. You will then play a mock game.

TAPING STUDIO ADDRESS: NBC Studios, 3000 West Alameda Boulevard, Burbank, California 91523

TAPING DAYS AND HOURS: Varies

NUMBER OF CONTESTANTS COMPETING/PLAYING: Three contestants compete against one another.

NECESSARY PLAYING SKILLS: A quick recall of broad general knowledge.

OBJECT OF GAME: You win money by first buzzing in and answering questions correctly. You must spend that money on prizes offered for sale at a fraction of their actual retail value. Whoever has the most money at the end of the game wins and gets to play the bonus round.

PRIZES AVAILABLE: More than $100,000 in cash and prizes.

COMMENTS: They are looking for self-confident, outgoing, and vocal players. Make yourself stand out by dressing nicely and having a funny or interesting introduction prepared. Be animated, speak up, and support other contestants who are trying out. Special week: Tournament of champions.

I PLAY THIS GAME: [ ] Very Well [ ] Well [ ] Okay [ ] Poorly

Scrabble

HOST: Chuck Woolery

PRODUCTION COMPANY: Reg Grundy

EXECUTIVE PRODUCER: Bob Noah

PRODUCER: Gary Johnson

CONTESTANT COORDINATOR: Beth Fiance

PHONE NUMBER: (213) 284-8644

INTERVIEW ADDRESS: 9911 West Pico Boulevard, Suite 520, Los Angeles, California 90035

INTERVIEW DATE AND TIME: Varies

INTERVIEW REQUIREMENTS: Your first interview will last approximately one hour, and there will usually be seventy-five to one hundred people auditioning with you. It will begin with a short (fifteen-clue) written test that is read aloud to you. Then you will be asked to stand up and speak for a couple of minutes about yourself. If you make the first cut, you will be invited back to play a mock game after being briefed on all the rules. Your second interview could last up to two hours. Once you are chosen, it could take one week to four months before you actually appear on the show.

TAPING STUDIO ADDRESS: NBC Studios, 3000 West Alameda Boulevard, Burbank, California 91523

TAPING DAYS AND HOURS: Varies, with five shows being taped each day.

NUMBER OF CONTESTANTS COMPETING/PLAYING: Two contestants compete against each other per game; four contestants per show.

NECESSARY PLAYING SKILLS: Skill at solving word puzzles.

OBJECT OF GAME: You must guess the words by filling in the blank spaces on an electronic Scrabble board with two letters at a time, which you draw at random. You will be given a clue and will be told how many letters will be in the word. If the letter chosen belongs in the word being played, it will drop into its correct position, and you will be able to make a guess or continue choosing letters. The winner of each round goes on to play the Sprint bonus round.

PRIZES AVAILABLE: Cash—no maximum amount, but you may only appear for five days.

COMMENTS: They are looking for friendly, animated, energetic, players who are good at word puzzles. Special weeks for college students, teens. Contestant searches throughout the U. S.

I PLAY THIS GAME: [ ] Very well [ ] Well [ ] Okay [ ] Poorly

SUPER PASSWORD

HOST: Bert Convy

PRODUCTION COMPANY: Mark Goodson

EXECUTIVE PRODUCER: Robert Sherman

PRODUCER: Joe Neustein

CONTESTANT COORDINATOR: Joyce Weiss Stevens

PHONE NUMBER: (213) 466-5103

INTERVIEW ADDRESS: 6430 Sunset Boulevard, Suite 1017, Hollywood, California 90028

INTERVIEW DATE AND TIME: Tuesdays through Thursdays; each interview lasts for two hours.

INTERVIEW REQUIREMENTS: You will be taught precisely how the game is played, and then you will play a mock game. Next, you will take a twelve-question written test involving word clues. Your second interview will consist only of a mock game.

TAPING STUDIO ADDRESS: NBC Studios, 3000 West Alameda Boulevard, Burbank, California 91523

TAPING DAYS AND HOURS: Saturdays, Sundays, and Mondays, 2:30 A.M. to 6:30 P.M., five shows a day.

NUMBER OF CONTESTANTS COMPETING/PLAYING: Two teams (one contestant and one celebrity) compete against each other.

NECESSARY PLAYING SKILLS: Good vocabulary and good communication skills.

OBJECT OF GAME: You must communicate a word to your partner, by use of a synonym or other one-word clue, within four seconds. Every time your team guesses the correct word, you will get a chance to solve the puzzle comprised of these "passwords." After the second round, the team with the most points will play "Cashword." You will receive three clues to help you guess the correct word. You will then switch celebrity partners and play two more rounds. Whichever team earns $500 first wins and goes on to play the bonus round.

PRIZES AVAILABLE: No limit—top winner has won $106,000.

COMMENTS: They are looking for bright, verbal, energetic people. You must watch and practice this game often for your interview. Dress nicely! Special weeks for tournament of champions, tournament of losers.

I PLAY THIS GAME: [ ] Very well [ ] Well [ ] Okay [ ] Poorly

WHEEL OF FORTUNE

HOST: Pat Sajak

EXECUTIVE PRODUCER: Merv Griffin

PRODUCER: Nancy Jones

CONTESTANT COORDINATORS: Harv Selsby, Scott Page, Peggy Lavell

PHONE NUMBER: (213) 520-5555

INTERVIEW ADDRESS: 1541 North Vine Street, 5th floor, Hollywood, California 90028

INTERVIEW DATE AND TIME: Varies

INTERVIEW REQUIREMENTS: Contestants will first take a written quiz consisting of fifteen puzzles. You must solve eight in order to pass. Those who pass stay in the room and play a mock version of the game. Then they stand and talk a little bit about themselves. After this, another cut is made. Those chosen are asked to come to a call-back. Your second interview, or call-back, will last close to 1½ hours, and you will be asked to play the game again in front of the coordinators and the associate producer.

TAPING STUDIO ADDRESS: NBC Studios, 3000 Alameda Boulevard, Burbank, California 91523

TAPING DAYS AND HOURS: Varies

NUMBER OF CONTESTANTS COMPETING/PLAYING: Three contestants compete against one another.

NECESSARY PLAYING SKILLS: Skill at solving puzzles containing popular phrases, people, and things.

OBJECT OF GAME: You must earn the largest amount of money by solving the various puzzles on the game board. You do this by picking consonants that fit into the puzzle. You will first spin the wheel to determine that consonant's dollar value. You will continue guessing consonants and/or buying vowels that fit into the puzzle (alternating with your two opponents), until you have enough money in your account to make it worthwhile for you to guess the phrase and then purchase any of the merchandise displayed.

PRIZES AVAILABLE: A wide variety of merchandise, including trips, boats, luggage, furniture, appliances, antiques, and jewelry, totaling over $117,000.

COMMENTS: They are looking for players with outgoing personalities. Special weeks for celebrities, couples, college students, teens. Contestant searches throughout the U.S.

I PLAY THIS GAME: [ ] Very well [ ] Well [ ] Okay [ ] Poorly

Do You Remember These Old Game Shows?

"Battle of the Ages"—This prime-time game show was a talent contest between a team of children and a team of adult celebrities.

"Brains and Brawn"—A game of physical and mental prowess that teamed an athlete with a celebrity.

"Do You Trust Your Wife?"—In 1956 Edgar Bergen, Charlie McCarthy, and others hosted this married couples' quiz show. In the fall of 1958 Johnny Carson did the honors, teaming up for the first time with a new announcer by the name of . . . you guessed it! Ed McMahon!

"E.S.P."—Vincent Price hosted this exploration into the phenomenon of extrasensory perception. Guests related personal experiences and also participated in various tests to demonstrate their unusual abilities.

"How's Your Mother-in-Law?"—Host Wink Martindale had a panel of three comedians joke about their mothers-in-law, and then decide which of the three contestants, each of whom *was* a mother-in-law, was the nicest or the "best."

"It Pays to Be Ignorant"—This was a forties spoof of game shows hosted by former radio-show disc-jockey Tom Howard. The celebrity panel had to try to *avoid* answering such stumpers as "What beverage is made from tea leaves?"

Chapter 2

Strategy: Selecting the Game Show That's Right for You

Now that you've reviewed your options, the next step is deciding which game(s) to tryout for. This is an important decision for two reasons:

1. Once you've been on a game show, you will have to wait at least a year before you can try out for another one;
2. You don't want to get on a show and then end up losing, if you can help it.

After my third game show win, I finally convinced my sister Lori to try out for a show. She wanted to be on "Sale of the Century" because she liked the game and all the wonderful prizes it offered. After my thorough prepping, she passed her interview and was chosen as a contestant. She was pitted against two other players. A trivia question was read by the host, and the contestant who buzzed in first got to answer.

My sister knew the answers to most of the questions, but unfortunately it took her a while to actually process that information in her mind and then press the buzzer. Had she been faster on the draw, she would have won the game. My sister is an excellent example of what happens when someone insists on playing a game they like and not one they're good at playing.

Everyone has a special skill, so you should look for shows where you can use your talents to their fullest potential. Recognizing your playing abilities will increase your chances of being selected as a contestant and your chances at winning. To get a good idea of the types of games currently on TV, watch as many different game shows as you possibly can. If a game appeals to you, watch it repeatedly. Understand it and play along. You might discover that there is more to it than you thought. Perhaps the main game is easy, but the "end game" or "bonus round" is very difficult.

"Jeopardy!," for example, is a game that is interesting to watch but very tough to play. Most people can only respond to a few of the categories offered. It takes keen knowledge retention and a fast hand on the buzzer to play "Jeopardy!" well. (See chapter 4 for buzzer pressing tips).

"One Million Dollar Chance of a Lifetime" might offer the highest stakes on television, but if you're not quick with word puzzles, put all that money out of your mind. You also won't have a chance if you're single, because they only use married couples as contestants.

GAME SHOW TYPES

Every few months you'll see game shows being canceled and new ones being added to the TV lineup. You'll also discover old shows (like "Match Game," "Concentration," "You Don't Say," and "Let's Make a Deal") being resurrected years after they go off the air. Though shows come and go regularly, there are essentially six types of games—General Knowledge, Skill, Logic and/or Luck, Talent, and Romance—and a few combinations of these six.

If a game shares two or more of these characteristics, it may be difficult to put it in a category. Try to evaluate it by the predominant skill required. "Wheel of Fortune," for example, does take a little luck and knowledge when it comes to spinning the wheel and understanding the phrase (though the phrases are usually familiar), but primarily it demands puzzle-solving capabilities, so you should classify it as a skill game. You could say that you need a little luck to win any game, but when it comes to general-knowledge or trivia-type games, first and foremost you must know the subject matter.

General-knowledge Games

Since trivia games require a good retention and quick recall of material from a wide variety of subjects, they are usually considered the most difficult. If you are good with general-knowledge questions, aim for shows that will allow you to tap your intellect, like "Sale of the Century," "Trivial Pursuit," "High Rollers," "Split Second," "Blockbusters," "Bullseye," or "Strike It Rich." If you are better with "soft" trivia, look for shows like "All Star Blitz" and "Hollywood Squares." These games ask easy social, arts, science, and entertainment-oriented questions. Vocabulary experts should look for games like "Word Play." A game like "Name That Tune" would be perfect for a music buff.

Game show aficionados have declared "Jeopardy!" the hardest all-around knowledge game on television. For the past twenty years its esoteric categories and obscure answers (formulated as questions) have truly made it the "Harvard" of cerebral game shows.

Skill Games

Many people find skill games to be the most challenging and the most fun. The skills called for involve solving puzzles; communicating words, phrases, or concepts (either visually or verbally); pricing merchandise; memorizing different items; and performing stunts.

If you enjoy solving puzzles containing familiar words, expressions, places, or people, you might want to try out for "Wheel of Fortune," "Scrabble," or "One Million Dollar Chance of a Lifetime." These games require quick visualization of the missing letters or words contained in a puzzle. They are very popular because there are usually easy phrases or words mixed in with the more difficult ones.

If you are proficient at giving and receiving word clues, try out for fast and exciting skill games like "Super Password" or "$25,000 Pyramid." These shows test your ability to come up with efficient synonyms and communicate them quickly. "Celebrity Charades" and Burt Reynolds's quick-sketch game "Win, Lose, or Draw" make competing fun and usually attract especially animated players.

Memory games are relatively simple to learn, but they usually involve other skills as well. If you have a sharp memory and are good at solving "symbol" puzzles, games like "Concentration" are the perfect arena in which to showcase your talents.

The two most popular merchandise-pricing games in the history of television game shows are "The Price Is Right" and "Let's Make a Deal." They require skills that many people possess; namely, pricing and buying everyday items for themselves, their families, and their homes. If you know a bargain when you see one, you might also want to try out for a fun, prize-valuing game like "Bargain Hunters."

Playing stunt games like "Truth or Consequences," "Beat the Clock," and "Treasure Isle" demands physical agility and a good sense of humor. If you have these qualities, you can count on having a good time, win or lose!

Logic and/or Luck

If you're a little rusty with history, geography, and other assorted trivia or just can't handle the pressure of skill games,

"Hollywood Squares" Host John Davidson

you should look for shows like "Liar's Club," "The New Newlywed Game," "Match Game," "Family Feud," or "Card Sharks," where luck and logic will be your major obstacles. Games of this type are perfect for first-time contestants because they are the easiest to play.

Talent

If you aren't good at crossword puzzles, word clues, or trivia but can sing or dance up a storm, you might consider competing on talent shows like "Star Search," "You Write the Songs," "The Gong Show," or "Dance Fever." Even if you can't sing, but you love to *pretend* you're performing, there's a show called "Puttin' on the Hits" that will give you the opportunity to lip sync your way into winning fabulous cash and prizes.

Romance

Are you searching for a new romance in your life? If you could use a little help from Cupid's arrow, check out "The Dating Game" or "The Love Connection." You won't win lots of money, but these games are fun to play; and who knows, you could meet the date of your dreams!

The Games Cupid Plays

HOST: "For $10,000 cash and a trip to the Bahamas, fill in the blank: 'Love and blank.' "
CONTESTANT: "Umm, Umm . . . Marriage!"
HOST: "Marriage is correct—you're a winner!"

Love and marriage are topics that always have and always will make for great game shows. We've said "I do" to games such as: "Wedding Party," "For Love or Money," "Matches and Mates," "Honeymoon Race," "Perfect Match," "Blind Date," "Chance for Romance," "The Newlywed Game," "The Dating Game," "The Love Connection," "Amateur's Guide to Love," "The Better Sex," "The Love Experts," "Do You Trust Your Wife?" and the hilarious "How's Your Mother-in-Law?"

PLAYING FACTORS

Now that you know what types of games are most accessible to you, weigh the playing factors working for and against you.

Timing

Every game has some type of timing element involved in its rules. If you will be racing against a time clock or trying to beat the best time of your opponent when answering a question, solving a puzzle, or communicating a word, you are going to have to hold up well under pressure.

Lisa Furubotten, contestant coordinator for "$25,000 Pyramid" and "$100,000 Pyramid," told me that many of the people who try out for her show watch and play the game for months in advance. Contestant hopefuls must practice communicating word clues in order to acquire the speed necessary just to compete, let alone win.

If you are playing games like "Sale of the Century" or "Jeopardy!," you need to buzz in first just to get the opportunity to answer before your opponent(s). If you aren't good at giving quick responses or feel that you might panic under the pressure of a time clock, stay away from these games.

Competition

Another factor to consider is how many contestants you will be competing against. Will there be one other player? Two? Four? In many cases, the less competition, the better your odds of winning.

Let's say, for example, that you are thinking of trying out for "Wheel of Fortune" because you are good at puzzles. If you were to consider your other puzzle-game options, "Scrabble" would be a better bet since there is only one other competitor. Now if you are saying to yourself, "Wheel of Fortune" is an easier game to play than "Scrabble," you are right. But remember, if it's easier for you, it will also be easier for your opponent(s).

In this particular situation, the luck element involved must also be considered. When playing "Wheel of Fortune" your puzzle-solving skills may go untouched if you land on "lose a turn" or "bankrupt." On "Scrabble" you don't have that risk;

Dick Clark, host of "$100,000 Pyramid"

all you need is a skill for visualizing incomplete words. Taking the competition and luck elements into account, try out for "Scrabble" first and "Wheel of Fortune" second so that you will take advantage of "Scrabble's" better odds. As you can see, you must be careful to compare apples to apples when deciding if the competition aspect of your game show choice makes a difference.

Partners

Have you ever thought about playing games like "The New Newlywed Game," "Dream House," "Strike It Rich," or "Family Feud" with your spouse or family? I made a point of choosing game shows where I alone was responsible for my being selected and winning or losing. My reasoning was that my husband or family might not have been able to attend all the interviews or might not have found the time to prepare properly for the game. I knew that if I was going to win, I had to do it on my own. I didn't want to be dependent on or disappointed with anyone but myself. I also did my homework and discovered that during that period of time game shows with single players offered more money and bigger prizes than those with couples or families. Today, with shows for couples like "One Million Dollar Chance of a Lifetime," the reverse is true!

When I look back on my first game show experience, I see that there was another side to the coin—my husband and I could have given each other moral support. We also could have kept each other company during the long hours of taping. If you would feel better playing with your family, by all means, try out for a couple or family game, but first make sure the other person(s) involved have the time and energy necessary for practicing, interviewing, and taping.

You must also decide if playing with a celebrity partner would help or hinder you. Here again, if they are not quite quick enough, you could suffer for it. But if they are top-notch players (and most of them are just that), you will only benefit from their abilities.

Dan and Laureen Crisafulli, happy millionaires after winning "One Million Dollar Chance of a Lifetime"

Games that use many celebrity players have pros and cons as well. A few contestants I've interviewed felt that some of the stars on "Match Game," "Hollywood Squares," and "All Star Blitz" were more interested in trying to amuse the audience than they were in giving the correct answers. I have seen it happen myself, so it is something to take into consideration when deciding what type of game to try out for.

PRIZES

The major network programs award anywhere from $2,500 to $1 million in cash and/or prizes to their winners. Some games offer prizes such as cars and furniture, while others only give away cash. When deciding what kind of prizes you want to win, take a good hard look at what you need in your life. If you need money, don't let the fact that a game show awards only prizes deter you. You can convert prizes into cash simply by selling them (see chapter 7).

Now, use your completed game show factsheets to aid you in targeting the shows that will give you the best chance of being chosen and winning with your particular skills. Study all the information on the factsheets, and narrow your selections down to the best three. Once you have pinpointed your first, second, and third choices, you can proceed to set up your interview appointments.

You may find yourself in a situation similar to this: you're attracted to the "$25,000 Pyramid" because it gives away a lot of cash, but the downside is that you're not as quick as you should be at communicating word clues. Your second choice is "The Price Is Right" because you are skilled at guessing the value of merchandise. But you need cash, and this show doesn't offer a lot of that green stuff. You now have to decide which show will give you the best opportunity to use your special talents and win the prizes you desire most.

In this instance I suggest making "$25,000 Pyramid" your second choice and trying out first for the show that you'll probably do better on—"The Price Is Right." You can always sell the prizes you don't want or need. If you don't get chosen for "The Price Is Right," sharpen up your word-communication skills and then try out for "$25,000 Pyramid."

If this is your first game show and you're a little "gun shy," try out for an easy game regardless of what the prizes are. That way you will gain the confidence needed to win big on the next game show you choose.

IMPROVING YOUR ODDS

You can increase your chances of being selected if you try out for a couple of game shows during the same period of time. If you demonstrate good contestant potential for more than one show, more than one may want to use you. If you have to wait a month before the taping of your first pick, but choice number two wants you next week, be patient and wait a month. You'll be glad you did, because you're bound to do better on the game show that's best suited to you.

Note: When you do try out for more than one show, *don't mention it to any of the show's coordinators*. I once heard a would-be contestant tell the coordinator that she had tried out for another game show a few days earlier. The coordinator was obviously disappointed and asked her how she could have tried out for another show when she seemed to want to be on her show so badly. What this "hopeful" didn't realize was that she was inadvertently telling the coordinator two things about herself: 1. she didn't really care what show she was on; and 2. she didn't feel confident enough to be chosen for either show.

Needless to say, the coordinator did not call that applicant back for a second interview. Most contestant coordinators are very loyal to their shows, and they tend to take things very personally. Although it is smart to try out for two shows at the same time, don't ruin your chances by flaunting that fact to a coordinator.

Chapter 3

Operations: Becoming a Contestant

People from virtually every ethnic, financial, geographical, and cultural background try out to become game show contestants. You don't need to be good-looking or smart to be chosen for most shows. Contestants come in all different shapes, sizes, and ages. Yet it is these ordinary people that make game shows so popular. As Monty Hall says, "There are no brighter stars than those that shine in the day!" Producers are looking for friendly, average people. If you are male, from out of town, (i.e., not from L.A.), a member of a minority group, or older than forty, you're in luck! Most shows have a tremendous shortage of people in these areas.

A lot of men would like to become contestants, but they don't try out because they don't have time. Of course, more women are working now than ever before, but they seem, on the whole, to have more flexible schedules, which allow them the time to interview. For this reason, you will see an average of five women to every man on most TV game shows.

Minorities are encouraged to try out because they add a "cultural spark" that producers and audiences find very appealing. Out-of-towners have a definite advantage because their taping sessions are granted sooner due to their limited stay. If you are just visiting L.A., most producers will interview, test, and tape you within a few days. During the peak vacation periods, shows try to use as many tourists as they possibly can. If you are over forty, you will certainly have a better chance of standing out since more young people tend to try out.

If you do *not* fit into one of these groups, fear not! There are still plenty of ways you can make yourself shine through the crowd.

If you have the time, go down to the studio and watch a game being taped before you try out for it. Getting accustomed to the set, cameras, lights, and so on will make you more comfortable when it's your turn to play.

Request audience tickets by writing a letter directly to the network that carries the show. It will take longer to receive your tickets if you write to the local station, because they will only forward your request to the parent network.

It is also possible to pick up the tickets at the studio, but do this early in the morning. If the show is very popular, or if it happens to be peak tourist season, those tickets will go extremely fast.

All game show tickets are free. Sometimes the show will even distribute tickets to pedestrians with the promise of free bus transportation to and from the studio for those who attend the taping. Nice door prizes are given away too, as an inducement for the audience to stay until the end of the show.

SETTING UP AN INTERVIEW

To get on a game show, the first thing you must do is call the show's contestant coordinator for an interview appointment. If you are from out of state and are planning a trip to Hollywood or New York City, you may also write requesting an interview.

It is *not* necessary to include a photo; a snapshot will be taken sometime during the interview. Calling, however, will get you a faster response, because many shows receive literally hundreds of requests for interviews by mail. When you telephone, you should be given an appointment date and time immediately.

Be polite and friendly when calling to set up your interview. It is the coordinator's job to weed out undesirables, and they can spot one a mile away—even over the telephone. Have your game show factsheets in hand so you can jot down such important information as how many interviews you'll have to attend, the days and times, how long they will last, what you should wear, and what tests, if any, will be given. Since some producers require you to attend up to four interviews—or one interview where you have to watch the taping of five shows first—it's crucial that you know exactly what you're getting into so that you can adjust your schedule.

Most game shows are filmed in Hollywood and Burbank, California. Ask for the address, directions, and parking instructions for the interviewing office or taping studio. There is nothing worse for the nerves than driving around for twenty minutes trying to find the office parking lot. Try to figure out exactly how long it will take to get to the interview so you can plan accordingly. Ask if there's a charge for parking in the lot. If there is, you can also inquire into the possibility and cost of parking on nearby streets.

If you are coming from out of town, call to confirm your interview or appearance date and time before you leave on your trip. Try to anticipate all your possible needs, and make a short list of questions. Plan on arriving ten to fifteen minutes before your scheduled interview. This extra time will permit you to visit the restroom so you can freshen up and compose yourself. It is extremely important to make a good first impression when you meet the contestant coordinator.

For a successful interview you should be absolutely at your best. If you aren't feeling great, or looking good, or if for some reason you can't make the interview on time, simply call to cancel and schedule a new one on another day; the coordinator will never hold it against you. Since they interview often it will be easy to find another time. This is your one shot—make sure you are properly prepared and in a good state of mind.

You may be at your interview for many hours, so remember to keep your energy level high. An in-studio interview usually occurs after many hours of filming, so use the taping breaks to stand up and stretch frequently. Bring along a piece of fruit or a candy bar for some quick energy before the coordinator starts interviewing the audience for possible contestants.

Even if you are looking and feeling great, it can be difficult to be selected as a contestant if you aren't familiar with the interview procedures. Here is a blow-by-blow description of what you can expect.

THE APPLICATION

Game show production companies will always give you an application form to fill out when you arrive. These forms are relatively simple to complete, but you can be disqualified instantly if you don't meet the eligibility requirements. Most applications will ask you for the following information:

Name: ______________________________
Address: ______________________________
Phone: (home) ______________ (office) ______________
Social Security No.: ______________________________
Date of Birth: ______________________________
Occupation: ______________ Marital Status: __________
List of other game show appearances with the dates the shows aired: ______________________________
Special interests and hobbies: ______________________
Are you related to, or friends with, any member of our production staff, network, station, sponsor, or ad agency? __________

If you don't have an office phone number, give them a second phone number where you can be reached or where they can leave a message. If you use a friend's, or family member's phone number, remember to let that person know about it.

It is very important that you list the correct air dates of any previous shows on which you've appeared. Every network and/or production company has their own restrictions regarding how many game shows you can be on and how often. The current rules are as follows:

1. You may not have appeared on another show which had its air date within the last twelve months. This means that even if you taped the show over a year ago, if it wasn't shown until last Tuesday, you will have to wait the full twelve months from the last Tuesday date before you can be on another game show. This restriction applies to every station and network.

   You might be able to swing an interview after only eleven months from your last appearance because you probably won't tape the new show until the twelfth month anyway. Just explain your eligibility problem to the coordinator or producer, and if they want to use you as a contestant, they will arrange it so that there will be no conflict.
2. Syndicated or network shows on CBS now permit three game shows in a ten-year period.
3. Syndicated or network shows on NBC will also grant you three game shows within a ten-year period.
4. Syndicated or network shows on ABC permit you to appear on two game shows within five years.
5. Independent stations have no set rules; they are left up to the individual production companies.

If you have past game show experience, be sure and check the show's and the station's current policies, and report the information accurately. This is mandatory because if it is discovered later that you have lied or made a mistake, you will have to forfeit all the money and prizes you've won.

Joyce Weiss Stevens, contestant coordinator for "Concentration," "Child's Play," "Super Password," and "Blockbusters," remembers a woman who got on "Joker's Wild" and "Concentration" within a short time of one another. Despite the wig and other assorted disguises she used, she was found out and had to forfeit the thousands of dollars and beautiful prizes she had won. A formal announcement was made explaining what this woman had done and why she had to return all of her winnings. As you can imagine, this televised punishment proved to be quite embarrassing.

So if you think you can get around these rules by changing your hair color or growing a mustache—forget it! Nowadays production companies have computers cross-checking all names with their Social Security numbers. If you do manage to slip by at first, there are many other ways producers can catch you, one of which is the viewing audience. It's absolutely amazing how often they will recognize contestants who have been on other shows and write in about them.

Many years ago, for example, my husband and I took a trip to New York. We were standing on the corner of 42nd Street and Broadway when a woman approached me and asked, "Didn't I see you on 'Match Game' a couple of years ago?" I just stared at her in total disbelief. That she could have remembered me from a show I played on many years ago in California astonished me.

Michael Hensley from Detroit, Michigan, won $10,400 on "Wheel of Fortune." A year after that appearance, he was sitting in the audience waiting for the taping of "Hollywood Squares" to end so he could try out to become a contestant, when along came the "Wheel of Fortune" contestant coordinator giving a tour of the studio to a group of hopefuls. The coordinator spotted Michael and asked him to come over to the group. He introduced him and told everyone, "This is a man who bought a lot of vowels when he played on the show." (When trying to solve a puzzle, "Wheel of Fortune" contestants are allowed to use any consonants, but to use vowels they must *pay* from their previous game earnings.) Mike was flabbergasted that the coordinator not only recognized him but remembered the way he played an entire year later.

So don't take any chances. It would be tragic to win $25,000 on a show only to have to return all of it because you didn't check the station's policy or you fudged on a past air date, even if only by a few months.

Many application forms will also ask you if you are a member of a performing union such as SAG or AFTRA. It has only been in the last few years that game shows have opened their doors to actors. You may feel that actors have an unfair advantage because they practice their speaking skills so often. The harsh truth is that more than 80 percent of all actors and actresses are unemployed, and 40 percent have never worked in television or movies. These statistics, combined with the fact that most actors don't play games any better than nonactors, leads one to conclude that they deserve the opportunity to try out for a game show too.

Your date of birth is requested because the majority of shows only use people over eighteen, except when they devote a week entirely to young children and teens. Most kids love the experience of being on a game show. If you have any children, you might ask the contestant coordinator when interviews will be held for these special shows.

Be sure to take advantage of the "special hobbies and interests" section on the application. Write about the most unusual things you can so that the coordinator will want to ask you about them later. Remember, you must make yourself stand out in the coordinator's mind if you want to have an advantage over the other would-be contestants.

If you know anyone on the show's staff, even if they just work in the cafeteria, you *must* disqualify yourself immediately. Now, when I use the term "know anyone," I mean someone with whom you are friendly. If you met someone on the staff very briefly, that person would be considered an acquaintance.

My friend Jennifer waited five months just to interview for the original "Hollywood Squares." When she went down to their offices, she recognized an old friend on the production set. Once they made eye contact, she knew it was over. Had she not mentioned this friend and gone on to win on the show, she would have had to return all the cash and prizes she won. She would also have been branded ineligible for any show produced by that company and possibly been blackballed from other game shows as well. Not answering this portion of the application truthfully is a big gamble that's definitely not worth the risk!

While filling out the application, you will undoubtedly notice that you are not the only one in the room. Some game shows interview 300 people at one time; others only 8. Don't be intimidated or discouraged by what appear to be difficult odds. If there are 30 applicants and all of them are great, they will use all 30. You are not actually competing against these people; you are just trying to make yourself stand out. So be friendly with these other hopefuls. The coordinator does not want to see contestants being rude or hostile toward one another.

After collecting your application, the coordinators or their assistants will take your picture, which will be attached to your application card. This photograph will help them remember who you are. A happy contestant is what they're looking for, so be sure to flash those pearly whites!

TESTING

Contestant coordinators and producers must test game show applicants to determine if they have what it takes to be contestants on their show. They can't afford to use contestants who don't "perform" well.

The Personality Test

Although every show's testing procedures are different, you will always receive some sort of "personality" test. You may be asked to stand up and say a few words about yourself, or

A large group of contestant-hopefuls taking a written test

you may be asked questions for up to fifteen minutes. Questions that are typically asked include: "Where were you born?" "What do you do for a living?" and "Do you have any hobbies or special interests?" Contestant coordinators and producers aren't necessarily concerned with what you do for a living or where you were born; they just want to see if you have what it takes to be a good contestant. Confidence, enthusiasm, sincerity, and friendliness are the key ingredients that coordinators are looking for. They can determine within a few minutes whether you are quiet and shy or the energetic, happy-go-lucky player they need for their show. Always have a brief introduction prepared (see "12 Tips for Achieving the Interview 'Edge,' " page 50).

The Written Test

Some shows require you to take a written test. It might consist of ten multiple-choice questions or fifty fill-ins. Each show's written test and grading scales are unique. "Hollywood Squares" and "Card Sharks" ask only a few logic and light trivia questions. "Wheel of Fortune" and "Scrabble" will have you solve anywhere from fifteen to thirty-one puzzles on popular expressions, people, things, and places. "Sale of the Century" 's test contains fifty moderately hard trivia questions, while "Jeopardy!" requires you to answer fifty very difficult knowledge questions. Some contestants found that the test for "Jeopardy!" was almost as rigorous as a college entrance exam.

These written tests are designed to reveal two things about you: 1. that you fully understand the concept of the game; 2. that you have the ability to solve puzzles and answer questions quickly and accurately.

The best way to prepare for a written game show test is to watch the show often to determine the types of questions and puzzles that are used. You can employ many of the techniques in chapter 4, "Game-playing Techniques," when taking your written test as well. Some contestant coordinators will change their test questions every few months to ensure that second-time applicants haven't already answered the questions and to cut down on people passing along the questions to their friends.

Here are some sample test questions to give you an idea of what you'll be facing. You will find more practice questions and puzzles in the Appendix. Remember: The more you practice, the better you'll do.

WORD CLUES

1. A man wears a wig or a ______________________

2. You see these in store windows: ________________

3. Lady = ______________________________

4. Monkey = ____________________________

PUZZLES

5. _ O L U _ _ _ _ E R

6. H _ R _

7. Some people stretch this to the limit. _ _ F _ Y

8. People just didn't buy it. E D _ E _

GENERAL KNOWLEDGE

9. The family name of Britain's rulers since 1917. ________

10. Some say the meat of this armored, plated mammal tastes like duck. ________

11. Type of business founded by Aaron N. Ward in 1872. ________

12. If you have one of these, your garden looks great but your hand looks awful. ________

Don't be afraid of having to take a written test. If you get a great score on your personality test, some coordinators will completely overlook low written-test scores, as long as you fully understand the game and are sincerely having fun playing it.

If you don't know the answer to a written-test question, guess! This applies to playing the mock (rehearsal) game as well. Producers want to know that your "wheels are spinning," regardless of whether you are right or wrong.

The Mock Game

The old saying, "It's not whether you win or lose that counts, but how you play the game" really holds true when playing a mock or rehearsal game. Winning or losing doesn't make a difference in determining whether you are chosen; *how* you win and lose does.

Coordinators will usually start by asking if there is anyone in the room who hasn't seen the game on TV. *Always* watch the

---

Answers **1.** Toupee **2.** Manikin **3.** Woman **4.** Ape **5.** Volunteer **6.** Hero **7.** Taffy **8.** Edsel **9.** Windsor **10.** Armadillo **11.** Mail-order catalog **12.** Green Thumb

Did You Know That . . .

* Phyllis Diller had her first television exposure as a contestant on Groucho Marx's game show "You Bet Your Life"? It was in the late fifties, and she was a very young and very skinny housewife. Groucho found her to be much funnier than she was smart, so he helped her get her start in show biz. Phyllis and Groucho later made comedy albums and appeared on variety shows together.

* Gene Rayburn of "Match Game" fame started his career as an NBC page in New York? He returned to the network years later but this time as the host of several of their game shows—the first being a show called "Choose Up Sides." Six years later he hit gold with the successful "Match Game."

* Wink Martindale knew Elvis Presley while they were both teenagers growing up in Tennessee? Wink worked at the radio recording studio where Elvis cut his very first record, "That's All Right Mama." Wink and Elvis remained close personal friends throughout their careers.

show beforehand. Don't worry if you aren't sure of all the rules; someone will review them briefly before you begin the mock game.

The coordinator may ask you to avoid certain words while playing. Try to brand those instructions into your mind. Some shows will tell you to say "boobs" instead of "breasts" or "whoopee" instead of "sex." If you slip and say an "off-limits" word during the interview, you can bet the coordinator will think twice before using you for the actual taping.

"All Star Blitz" contestant coordinator Tony Pandolfo suggests answering all questions and solving all puzzles with confidence. Why should you answer a question with conviction when you know there's no way in the world that your answer is correct? Because the producers like to see emotion. If you're wrong, you will appear disappointed, and everyone will be able to sympathize with you. So answer as though you were sure, even if you feel hesitant: it makes for a more exciting game.

Don't be too serious a competitor or too sore a loser. If you're losing the practice game, you should appear to be enjoying yourself anyway. Laugh at your mistakes, and you will have a better chance of being selected. If you win the mock game—great! But don't expect to win any prizes. A mock game is merely a rehearsal to see how well you know and play the game.

While waiting your turn, you may be watching other hopefuls play. Show enthusiasm. If somebody wins, react positively. If somebody misses a question, react sympathetically. The producer and coordinator keep their eyes on everyone, so why not score a few points with them even when you're not actually "up at bat."

A disappointed "Tic Tac Dough" contestant misses a question

Winning and losing are both part of game shows. If you have fun playing the game, the producer will know the audience at home is enjoying watching and rooting for you. Thom McKee, a "Tic Tac Dough" contestant who won over $300,000 in cash, eight cars, and many more prizes, has said that the most fun for him was not winning all the cash and prizes, or even the television exposure, but playing the game! Try to keep this attitude in mind during your interview.

ELIMINATION

If you score *very* poorly on the written test or just can't maintain a high energy level, you will probably be eliminated. I can't stress enough how important it is for you to be "up" for all your interviews. Nobody wants to watch a dull person; that is why all game shows look for contestants with pizzazz!

Most coordinators start eliminating after the first introductions, written test, or short mock game. They do this by calling off the names of those who have made the first cut; the rest of the applicants are excused. It's very exciting when they call only a few names to stay and yours is one of them!

If you are asked to play a mock game with the producer, associate producer, or director in attendance during your first interview, congratulate yourself! You have definitely made it past the first cut. Now all you have to do is keep up your enthusiasm and have fun playing the game.

CALL BACKS

Those who make it past the eliminations are "called back" for more testing or interviews. Call backs may be conducted on the day of your first interview or up to four weeks later. Your second interview usually won't last as long as your first since you won't have to fill out an application or be advised of the rules. If you are from out of town, the coordinator will make every effort to schedule any follow-up interviews to coincide with your visit.

TV Game Show Believe It or Not!

Ida Mae McKinzie, contestant coordinator for the original "Hollywood Squares," tells the story of an elderly man who wrote to her requesting a chance to appear on the show so that he could impress everyone at his retirement home. Ida called him down and found him to be a cute, lovable old guy and chose him to play.

The gentleman played very well during the interview, but during the actual taping he picked squares that had already been taken and disagreed with celebrities who obviously knew the correct answers.

To the chagrin of everybody on the staff and in the audience, this man somehow ended up winning $30,000.

At the close of the show, Ida discovered that the man was almost completely deaf during the filming. He hadn't heard any of the questions, except those where he had read lips. Most of the time he just guessed at every question. The man told Ida, "I had to take out my hearing aid before the game started so I would look my best for the ladies back at the home."

When interviewing for the second or third time, try to say and do the same things you did the first time around. They obviously liked your presentation enough to invite you back, so don't spoil a good thing. You will do well on your call backs as long as you use the three E's: Enthusiasm! Energy! Emotion!

12 TIPS FOR ACHIEVING THE INTERVIEW "EDGE"

Now that you know what to expect at your interview, let's get down to the nitty gritty: how you can be selected! These tips are so important that each one could be the deciding factor in whether or not you become a contestant. Please read them carefully. After you've gone through them once, go back and read them again to make sure you haven't missed anything.

1. *Do your homework.* Watch every game show you interview for as many times as possible before the actual audition. Study them until you are *totally* familiar with the way they are played. The contestant coordinators are not going to teach you their game when you arrive at your interview; they will be evaluating how well you play it already. Any producer will tell you that when evaluating would-be contestants, they pay close attention to "knowledge of the game."

   Study the contestants on TV. Observe their appearance and behavior closely. Each game show tends to use a certain type of player. Some use serious-looking people; others use very excitable, vivacious people. Don't feel that you need to be a clone of what you see on TV. But, if the players are more serious and less likely to jump up and down every time they answer correctly, that's how you should behave at the interview.

   A good way to focus on player traits for a particular show is to list a few of each contestant's characteristics and then compare them. Soon it will be obvious what *type* of player the show is using.
2. *Prepare an introduction.* You will *always* be asked to say a few words about yourself. It may be in front of the other hopefuls and the coordinator, or in front of the contestant coordinator and the producer. Since speaking before a group of people is a common phobia, this will probably be by far the most difficult part of your interview and the area where the majority of people are eliminated.

   Breeze through this troublesome part of the selection process by having a short introduction ready in your mind. Most of the other hopefuls will not be prepared, so you will have a definite advantage over the others. Although you are not competing directly against the other applicants, the fewer people worthy of serious consideration, the better you're going to look.

Be prepared to elaborate if the producer asks you any questions, but try to keep your speech interesting. Talk about any unusual hobbies, passions, or significant events in your life. Don't talk about how nervous you are—everybody's in the same boat! On the four game shows I interviewed for, no one who spoke about his or her nervousness made it past the first cut.

I talked about my two jobs—court-reporting and gag writing—because they aren't too common. At one tryout, I spoke about my twin sister and my recent wedding engagement. I also laughingly told a producer that I have two standard poodles who think they are human.

Talking about collecting poisonous snakes as a hobby is more likely to catch the coordinator's attention than saying, "I am happily married to my wonderful husband and I have three wonderful children." Don't get me wrong—that information is nice and wholesome. Just try to add something funny or unique about your life so you will stand out from the crowd. If you can't think of any hobbies or interests, use your sparkling personality to convince them you'd make an excellent contestant.

When Steve Ray tried out for "All Star Blitz," he told the coordinator about his very unusual hobby—collecting dirt. It all started when his pen pal from New Zealand sent him an envelope full of homegrown dirt. He got such a kick out of it that he asked his other pen pals from around the world to do the same. His most treasured dirt came from the grave of John F. Kennedy the day he was buried. That little story, without a doubt, made Steve Ray stand out. He was chosen to play and went on to win $25,000 in cash and $4,000 in prizes.

Coordinators try to create a multi-regional feeling for the show, so if you are from out of town, take advantage of your "tourist" status. If you live nearby but were born in another state or country, go ahead and boast about it. Tell the contestant coordinator something like, "I am a native of Maine currently living in L.A." to add a new dimension to your image.

Avoid talking about your antique car or collection of original impressionist paintings. Producers know from experience that the audience will be more supportive of needy players—like a newly married couple, a pregnant woman, or a man with four children. It's hard to cheer for a contestant who flaunts the fact that he or she is already wealthy.

Never tell the coordinator that you're unemployed, sick, going through a divorce, or any other "downer." They want contestants who appear happy and unencumbered, not people who cry about their personal problems!

Try to speak from the heart, be honest, but don't feel you have to tell them a saga of your life and personal affairs. A little humor goes a long way: tell a funny story and don't be afraid to laugh at yourself. The point of your introduction is to show the coordinator and producer that you are a sincerely friendly player and that you won't freeze up when speaking in front of the cameras.

3. *Rehearse your introduction.* The best way to ensure a good "performance" is to rehearse your introduction beforehand. Rehearsals are not just for beginners. Successful people always rehearse before an important meeting or interview, at least mentally if not out loud. Think about the points you want to make, the impression you want to create, and the results you want to achieve with your introduction.

Rehearse your short speech in front of a mirror or ask a friend or family member to play the role of interviewer and go through a mock audition—everything

"Tic Tac Dough" champ Thom McKee shares a funny story with a competitor during a taping break

from shaking hands to talking about your hobbies. Afterward, discuss your performance. Your friend or family member may have some suggestions or constructive criticism for you. If possible, run through the entire process again afterwards to firm it up in your mind.

Speak slowly and clearly and try to enunciate. If you generally talk fast, practice slowing down your speech. If you have a soft, weak voice, practice speaking louder. Don't shout or yell, but speak up. It may help to pretend that you're speaking to a person at the far end of the room.

Rehearse in whatever way works best for you, but don't try to wing it!

4. *Take care with your appearance.* The coordinator's first impressions of you are extremely important. Don't wear any holey, wrinkled, or faded clothing. Women may wear pants but should stay away from shorts, tube tops, tank tops, sexy blouses, or any outfit that is too tight. They should also avoid wearing too much makeup or jewelry.

Men should avoid sweatclothes, T-shirts, shorts, sandals, and faded jeans. Wearing a suit and tie to the interview isn't mandatory, but they do create a polished look.

Fifteen-thousand-dollar "Press Your Luck" winner Ann Caulkins from Louisville, Kentucky, noticed that the interviewees who dressed like they were going to the beach never made it past the first cut. Sue Hensley, a winning contestant from Santa Monica, California, who appeared on "Joker's Wild," "All Star Blitz," and "Liar's Club," suggests: "Have your hair and makeup neatly arranged and dress with a casual, well-put-together look. You never have a second chance to make a first impression!"

One of the easiest ways to be noticed in the contestant crowd is to wear bright, lively colored clothing. Cheerful (not fluorescent or wild) colors will help convey the message that you are a fun-loving, happy individual. If you have a hat that coordinates well with your outfit, by all means, wear it. And, if you are in a branch of the military or were in one in the past, and have a uniform, use it to your benefit. The audience (and producers) greatly respect people who have served their country.

Proper grooming is essential. Your hair should be clean and neat. You might want to get your hair trimmed if it's on the long side. Dan Smith, a contestant hopeful who tried out for "$25,000 Pyramid," told me that he wasn't chosen because he knew his hair was way too long and his outfit way too flashy. He was greatly disappointed, because he played the mock game very well. It is a good idea to avoid any possible appearance problems by dressing conservatively.

5. *Eat something beforehand*. Never interview on an empty stomach. A growling tummy will distract you, not to mention the coordinator, and it is important to keep your energy up. If you have eaten onions or garlic for lunch, use a mint or breath spray. I know this might sound trivial, but bad breath may make you less appealing.

   Do not come to your interview "under the influence." All the staff needs to do is to see you the slightest bit "high" and you'll be out the door quicker than you can answer the question, "When was the war of 1812?" Alcohol and drugs won't help steady your nerves and your ability to think is diminished.

6. *Leave your bad habits at home*. If you are a nail biter, mustache stroker, hair twirler, gum chewer, or finger tapper, make a conscious effort to stop, if only for the duration of the interview. These are all characteristics of a nervous person and will not help you to appear confident and in control.

7. *Feel confident*. The coordinator will sense immediately if you are introverted or doubtful. Show that you're sure of yourself but don't overdo it. These "pros" can see right through someone who is acting. They don't want to be entertained by contestants; they want self-assured individuals who enjoy playing games.

8. *Don't act like a know-it-all*. If you know how to play the game well, don't laugh at those who obviously haven't done their homework. Nobody likes someone who's cocky. Be tactful, and no matter what the coordinator or producer tells you, don't contradict them (especially in front of the other contestants).

9. *Posture is important*. Stand and sit up straight. Poor posture is a no-no. If you slouch or slump in your

chair, you will tend to look tired and unenthusiastic about what's going on. Try to appear alert and ready for anything they throw your way.

10. *Be attentive*. Don't talk or whisper during the interview unless you are being questioned. If you do, the coordinator will feel that you aren't paying attention and don't really care about being chosen. And, you may miss an important instruction.

    Beverly Pomerantz, contestant coordinator for "One Million Dollar Chance of a Lifetime" and "The Dating Game," told me a story about a great-looking couple who wouldn't stop talking to each other while she was interviewing the other contestants. Though they played the game well, she decided not to use them because she couldn't take the risk that they would disrupt the filming of the game with all their whispering.

11. *Be friendly*. Shake hands with the coordinator and the producer. Look them right in the eye and smile. Mark Goodson, producer of countless game shows, likes to see "outgoing, enthusiastic, and naturally effervescent" people play on his show. If you aren't a happy or positive person by nature, there's never a better time than the present to change. In chapter 5, "Playing to Win," there are some great positive-thinking and confidence-building exercises to start you off.

    It may help to think of yourself as auditioning for a part in a movie. Practice smiling, looking happy, and, above all, appearing eager. Coordinators can often decide within a few minutes of meeting you whether you are right for their game, regardless of how well you score on the written test!

12. *It's okay to be nervous*. Unless you are truly exceptional, you will be nervous at your interview. Your hands will be sweaty, your pulse will quicken, you'll get goose bumps on your arms, and you'll have but-

terflies in your stomach. You may even forget some of the things you practiced saying. Don't worry. Producers expect people to be a bit jittery, and they allow for it. Ron Greenberg, producer of "Who, What, or Where," "Dream House," and the original "Sale of the Century," says, "Even though the minute you cross that threshold, you are being studied, we want to like you and choose you as a contestant."

If you follow these twelve tips you will certainly appear exceptional next to the average person who walks in the door. And you should come out of your interview as a contestant!

A WORD ABOUT CONTESTANT COORDINATORS

A contestant coordinator's job is comparable to that of a casting director; they see thousands of hopefuls a month and have the ever-painful task of rejecting the majority.

The main reason for the large turnover is that most would-be-contestants don't know what to expect at the interview; so they come totally unprepared. Most coordinators are bothered by that fact because they know people would do better if they knew the ground rules ahead of time. And if that were the case, they wouldn't have to interview as often, because they could use more people from each group of applicants.

Despite that fact their jobs can be quite frustrating. I have found coordinators to be great people. Their love of games is reflected in their devotion to their jobs, and the enthusiasm they have for their shows is always contagious. Many of them started out as contestants too, so they can relate to you extremely well.

Coordinators know just how to make your experience enjoyable and memorable. They love it when someone they have selected as a contestant wins big. And why not? They're the one who picked you, briefed you, rehearsed you, comforted you, advised you, congratulated you, consoled you, and escorted you through every aspect of the game. Coordinators and contestants can and often do become fast friends.

You can help them look good in their job by studying the guidelines in this chapter. Production staffs are always looking for the "perfect game show contestant," and if you play well (win or lose), it will mean a feather in the coordinator's cap because he or she had the insight to select you.

Game Show Trivia Quiz

1. What famous female newscaster was a prize model on an early New York game show in the fifties: ______________

2. On what popular game show in the fifties did an otherwise unemployed actor named James Dean work? ______________

3. True or false? Both Burt Reynolds and Tom Selleck were on "The Dating Game." ______________

4. What game show launched Pee Wee Herman's comedic career? ______________

5. Which of the following is not a game show?
   a. "Amateur's Guide to Love"
   b. "The Better Sex"
   c. "The Love Experts"

Answers: 1. Barbara Walters! She assisted emcee Sandy Becker on NBC's "Ask the Camera."
2. Dean used to test out the stunts for "Beat the Clock." Years later, when he became a superstar, he would often visit the set. He liked to see his old friends and eat the commissary's rice pudding.
3. True! Believe it or not, they both failed to win dates!
4. "The Gong Show"
5. They all were! "Amateur's Guide to Love" was hosted by Gene Rayburn in 1972, "The Better Sex" was hosted by Sarah Purcell and Bill Anderson in 1975, and "The Love Experts" was hosted by Bill Cullen in 1978.

CONGRATULATIONS!

If you have read and followed all the instructions and advice up to this point, you will no doubt receive a letter and/or phone call within a week or two after your interview(s), congratulating you on being selected. Go ahead and scream with delight—you've earned it!

Each game show I tried out for got back to me within four days. They will rarely let you know if you've made it on the day of your interview, unless they plan on using you for that week's taping.

Once you have been selected, your card and photograph will be put into the "good file" of desirable contestants. From this stack the producer will decide who will tape and when. The coordinator will call you later to set up the taping. Again, if you are a visitor from out of town, the show will make every effort to get you on quickly.

Most "Congratulations" letters use words to the effect of "You have been invited down to the studio for taping." This particular language conveys the message that they *intend* to use you, but they can't say exactly *when*, and in some rare cases, *if*, they will use you.

It may seem unfair to have to spend many hours interviewing and getting ready for the taping and then end up not being chosen to play. But the producer does have the right to change his mind if he feels you won't do his show justice. Maybe you aren't the same person he interviewed a couple of months ago, physically or emotionally. If you look and act in the studio like you did at the interview(s), however, chances are good that you will get to play.

Bear in mind that all shows overbook contestants. This is done in case someone gets sick, doesn't show up, or the game finishes earlier than expected and they end up going through a lot of players. It can also happen that two people look too much alike on a given day or someone breaks out in hives before the taping begins. Anything is possible, so be prepared. You might have to come back the next day or even the next week. See chapter 6 for more specific information on taping procedures and how producers choose who plays and when.

I was told the story of a woman who had to go back for six different tapings held on six consecutive weekends. She was very frustrated while waiting, but when she finally was chosen to compete, she played for three days straight and ended up winning a grand total of $22,000 in cash!

It is usually the producer, not the coordinator, who makes the final decision as to who will play and when, so don't call the coordinator to find out when you'll be on unless you have a very good reason. They are always busy interviewing new contestants, and you certainly won't chalk up any brownie points by calling and bugging them about your taping date.

In my experience, there are only two reasons to call at this stage. My friend Ellen received a "Congratulations" letter and a personal phone call from the coordinator telling her how great she was and how they would probably use her within the month. A few months went by and she still had not heard from the show. I advised her to call the coordinator to find out why she had not been asked to come down to film. She did, and it turned out that the assistant coordinator had lost her card. They were thrilled that she called; they had wanted to use her right away but didn't have a way to let her know.

The other appropriate time for a phone call is when you are going on a long trip and would like the coordinator to call when you return. The bottom line is: don't call unless it has been more than four months since you received your letter or you will be out of town for an extended period of time.

TRY, TRY AGAIN

If you don't make it past the first cut or don't receive a "Congratulations, you've been selected!" letter or phone call within a month after your interview, you can safely assume you didn't make it. It won't do you any good to phone the coordinator to ask why you were not chosen. They simply don't have the time or the heart to reveal everyone's flaws.

But don't be discouraged or traumatized because they felt you weren't right for their game. Learn from the interview experience. Read *Be a TV Game Show Winner!* again, renew your energy, and try out for the next show you chose. Or, if you're really determined to get on choice number one, wait the required period (anywhere from three to nine months) and try out again.

"One Million Dollar Chance of a Lifetime" contestant coordinator Beverly Pomerantz told me about a nice couple she selected who actually went on to win one million dollars. When the taping ended, they confided that they had been turned down by "every game show on TV" before they tried out for "One Million Dollar Chance of a Lifetime." Obviously, perseverance does pay!

The first time Cheryl Reinwand tried out for "$25,000 Pyramid," she didn't make it past the first cut. Cheryl felt she knew exactly why she wasn't chosen: she'd been shy, felt unfamiliar with the interview process, and was just not quick enough to impress the coordinator and producer.

But Cheryl would not give up; after six months she tried out again. During that time she wrote down every category and every word used on the show and practiced them every day with her husband and friends. Not only did she get on, but she sharpened her skills so much that she ended up playing the game for five straight days, winning $43,000 in cash. She then went on to compete on the "$100,000 Pyramid," where she won the $100,000 and a trip to the Fiji Islands, winning a grand total of $150,000.

So remember, keep studying the game. Try to reconstruct in your mind what went on during the interview. Were you "up" enough? Did you appear confident? Did you play the game well? Reevaluate your performance as best you can. Perhaps you weren't quite your best that day. Maybe your mind was preoccupied with other things. You can feel confident that the second time around you'll be more familiar with the game and the testing procedures.

You'll still be a winner even if you don't make it past the

first interview stage because you will probably make several friends along the way. There's a special rapport, a certain camaraderie that develops between people who are trying out for or playing on a game show, which causes them to bond quickly. There are lots of ex-contestants (winners and losers) who like to meet once a week just to watch their favorite game shows together. I've always felt that these friendships alone are worth the effort.

Chapter 4

Game-playing Techniques

It's fun playing on a game show, but naturally it's even more exciting when you win. Listed below are special game-playing techniques that will reduce your margin of error and give you a definite edge over your opponents.

WATCHING

Watching the game that you will be playing often will be of tremendous help to you. You will be more comfortable with the rules and quicker at playing in the studio if you study the way the game is played on TV.

Sense the proper flow of the game as you are playing along. Notice which letters are used most often by contestants when solving puzzles, what kind of body language is used to communicate words or phrases, and the time allotted for each question and round. Study the type of buzzer you will be pushing. If you have a VCR, you might want to tape a few shows so that you can observe all the different elements at your leisure.

It is also helpful to watch other game shows that call for the same skills needed in the game you are going to play.

STUDYING

After watching the game several times, you will have a good idea of the type of material the show uses for its questions and puzzles. Check out a few relevant books from the library, such as an almanac, encyclopedia, book of lists, thesaurus, or dictionary of synonyms. Read up on old sayings and popular expressions. To learn more about people, places, and things, read newspapers and browse through magazines such as *Time, Newsweek, People,* and *Psychology Today*.

If you watch shows like "Joker's Wild," "Bullseye," or "Jeopardy!" often, you will notice that they use many of the same subjects or categories repeatedly. Take advantage of this fact by studying those subjects in which you are especially weak. You will need to remember events, dates, people, and places quickly for games of this type, so study hard! Try to be aware of everything that's going on in the world today: art, music, sports, entertainment, current affairs. The more you study, the sharper you'll be for the game.

PRACTICING

If you are playing along with a word game like "Pyramid" or "Password," practice using different synonyms. You should be able to come up with three different synonyms to describe each word or phrase quickly. For example, good synonyms for the word "comfort" would include "console," "help," and "reassure." Practicing your word-communication skills often will help you develop the smooth and speedy answering flow that is crucial to winning this type of game.

Working on crossword puzzles and acrostics is a good way to get into the mode for puzzle games like "Chance of a Lifetime," "Scrabble," "Wheel of Fortune," "Chain Reaction," and "Concentration." Playing the old children's game "Hangman" will also hone your skill at solving word puzzles.

Although "Concentration" is primarily a puzzle-solving game, it also requires a sharp memory. Few people are born with great memories; most of us have to work at it. A good mind-honing exercise is to lay out, face down in even rows, a preshuffled deck of playing cards. Turn over two cards at a time, study their placement, and then turn them back over. The object of this exercise is to remember where the like-numbered cards are placed. When you match two cards, remove them from the table and continue turning over two cards at a time until you have matched the entire deck.

General-knowledge shows can be difficult to practice for since they use such a broad range of questions. To increase your knowledge of trivia, you must practice learning new information and retaining it. Watch shows like "Jeopardy!," "Sale of the Century," "Bullseye," "High Rollers," and "Trivial Pursuit," and quiz yourself on the various categories and subjects offered along with the other contestants.

If you will be playing a charade-type game, physically practice giving and receiving clues for popular phrases and book and movie titles with your family and friends. Use clear and concise body movements to convey your clues. A good charade player will use special gestures to communicate frequently used words like "the," "in," and "of." You will learn to recognize these often-repeated words simply by studying the show.

If you want to try out for a merchandise-pricing game like "Let's Make a Deal," "The Price is Right," or "Bargain Hunters," watch the show often, because many of the same items are used month after month. You will learn what washers, dryers, stereos, vacations, and cars are selling for and will be able to make an intelligent bid without going over the actual retail price. Also, study the prices of different types of merchandise in newspaper ads and consumers catalogs. The prices of smaller items like food and personal goods are easy to learn, and you can test yourself every time you go to the supermarket.

Whatever type of game you have chosen to play, you should have your family and friends test you by making up their own clues, puzzles, or questions from your various study aids. "Jeopardy!," "Sale of the Century," "The Price Is Right," "Scrabble," "Pyramid," "Password," "Chance of a Lifetime," and

"Wheel of Fortune" all have home board versions that make excellent practice tools as well. These games can be found in most toy and department stores.

If you will be entering a talent competition on a show like "Star Search," "You Write the Songs," "Puttin' on the Hits," "The Gong Show," or "Dance Fever," you'll need to have your routine down pat, so practice, practice! It takes a high-quality performance to impress the judges enough to award you first place. Participants on the above shows have told me they practice months, and sometimes even years, in advance.

BUZZING IN

If you are playing a game that requires you to beat another player to the answer by pressing a button or buzzer, you must act quickly. Do this by keeping your hand close to the buzzer at all times. Hold your fingers close together and keep your palm flat when you are pressing down so you won't miss the button in your excitement to answer.

You might find that using both hands when pressing a buzzer or button is easiest for you. There are two ways to do this: right-handers, place your right hand completely over the top of your left hand and then press down; left-handers do the reverse. This will ensure that your stronger hand is supplying the most pressure (and thus the quickest reaction) to the buzzer. You can also join your hands together (as if you were praying) and interlace your fingers. Once your fingers are intertwined, keep your palms flat, parallel, and close to the buzzer. The best way to decide what pressing technique is most comfortable for you is to experiment with all of them.

If the subject of the question sounds familiar but you aren't *quite* sure of the answer, press the button anyway. This will give you a few seconds to think of the full, correct answer. Waiting even a couple of seconds to firm up the answer in your mind before you press will give your opponent the opportunity to beat you at the buzzer. If the game deducts points or money for a wrong answer, use this strategy sparingly. Only react quickly if you are at least semi-certain of the answer.

ANSWERING

Answering a question, solving a puzzle, or communicating a word properly can be difficult. These tips will help you to answer better and faster.

Listen very carefully to the question or the clue. Immediately after hearing it, you should repeat it to yourself so it is correctly planted in your mind. If you know the answer, press the buzzer—but before saying it out loud, take a couple of seconds to repeat it in your head. I am sure you have seen situations in which contestants look as though they know the correct answer, but when they finally say it, it comes out wrong or backward. It happens all the time.

The other day, while watching "Jeopardy!," I saw a contestant blurt out, "What is a moss gathers no rolling stone?" Everyone chuckled, including her, although she must have been upset with herself for having said the answer backward. One of her opponents jumped on the buzzer and, naturally, answered the question correctly.

Be careful that you don't inadvertently give away a part of the answer to your opponent because you haven't thought it out thoroughly. If your opponent has no idea what the answer is and you say "The ace of spades" instead of "The eight of spades," you will have given away practically the entire solution.

When games such as "Wheel of Fortune," "Jeopardy!," or "One Million Dollar Chance of a Lifetime" ask for a place, don't limit yourself to just thinking of states, countries, or cities. The answer could be a college, monument, forest, or park. "Wheel of Fortune" winner Cary Schorr became completely stumped when she was given the clue "place" and a puzzle that looked like this "_ R _ N _ _ T _ N _ N _ _ _ R S _ T _." Even after she had accumulated

Did You Know That . . .

* Presidents Nixon, Ford, Carter, and Reagan have all appeared as guests on TV game shows? Reagan, first as an actor and then as governor, guest-starred on ''What's My Life?,'' ''I've Got a Secret,'' ''The Celebrity Game,'' and many others during the fifties, sixties, and seventies. Richard Nixon, then Vice President, appeared on the show ''Your First Impression,'' hosted by TV-favorite Monty Hall in the early sixties. And Ford (while congressman) and Carter (while governor) both appeared on ''What's My Line?'' in the seventies.

* ''Love Connection'' and ''Scrabble'' host Chuck Woolery wrote a top-ten country hit for country singer Tammy Wynette? Woolery's country roots were planted in Nashville, Tennessee, long before game shows became a way of life for him.

* Football great O.J. Simpson, rock star Alice Cooper, Agent 007 Roger Moore, and The Monkees all made their first TV appearances on ''The Hollywood Squares,'' then hosted by Peter Marshall?

* Bob Eubanks was responsible for bringing the Beatles to the ''Hollywood Bowl?'' Eubanks was working as a disc-jockey back in 1964 when he mortgaged his home for $25,000 to finance an American visit of a then-unknown group called the Beatles.

a lot of money and was given almost all the letters, she still lost the puzzle to another player because, as she puts it, ''I was on the wrong wavelength—I only thought about cities and states.'' (The answer was Princeton University.)

Sometimes the category heading will provide a clue to the answer. For example, a category entitled ''Bird-Brain'' might refer to people having a type of bird as part of their last name. Listen for key words or phrases contained in the question. Do your best to use logic in determining what that word or phrase could possible mean.

If a game gives you a choice of subjects to choose from, always select the narrowest category that you feel sure of. A category entitled "Caribbean Islands" is much easier to handle than one called "White Things," which is a heading that could include anything from cottage cheese to wedding dresses. If you are near the end of a round or are playing the bonus game, choose a familiar category so that you can quickly increase your score before the buzzer sounds.

Remember to phrase all your answers in the proper fashion. If you are playing the "$25,000 Pyramid" bonus round, you must answer, "Things having to do with . . ."On "Jeopardy!" you must begin your answer with a question like, "What is a . . . ?" On "Super Password" you may only give one-word clues.

Some shows allow you to give an answer even before the clock starts or the word or phrase is spelled out. Anticipating the answer could give you a big advantage. "Press Your Luck" contestant Will Dent accumulated $12,000 in his game account because he jumped in to answer the questions before host Peter Tomarken could even finish asking them.

Many games will also credit you for correct answers given to previous questions and clues. Let's say that you are playing "Pyramid." You can't guess the word so you pass it, but the answer suddenly dawns on you while your next clue is being given. If you guess the answer correctly, even though you're on another clue, you will be given credit for it.

When asked the price of certain items on shows like "Let's Make a Deal," "Bargain Hunters," or "The Price Is Right," be careful not to overbid. I once saw a "Price Is Right" contestant bid $24,000 on a showcase containing scuba gear, water skis, fishing rods, clothing, and a one-week trip to the Bahamas. Host Bob Barker even asked the contestant if she wanted to change her answer. She stood firm on her bid and lost miserably. The woman later explained to Bob that she hadn't done a lot of traveling, so it was difficult for her to guess the price of that showcase. If you aren't certain of a price, bid lower rather than higher so that you will still be in the running should your opponent overbid.

You might be asked questions that seem unbelievably easy. Don't make the mistake of thinking they are trick questions. Ninety-nine out of one hundred questions are not tricky. When "All Star Blitz" player Steve Ray saw the phrase "Girls blank blank blank blank blank," his first instinct was to say "Girls just want to have fun." He thought that was too obvious, so he didn't attempt to solve it. His opponent immediately gave the same answer and won the round.

Keep in mind the fact that producers want you to win. They are not out to give you very difficult or trick questions—it makes them look bad and the show appear very dull. Art Alisi, producer of "High Rollers," "Bargain Hunters," "PDQ," "Hollywood Squares," and "Gambit," says, "Whether you are playing on a game show or just living life, go with your first instincts—they are usually the best."

Finally, one of the most important answering tips: don't waste precious time staring at the time clock. Many contestants lose the game because they become distracted or pressured into answering. Try to focus on the question and keep the time clock in the back of your mind only.

SOLVING PUZZLES

Initially, when trying to figure out a puzzle, use a vowel (if permitted) or work on revealing the first letter of the word. This will aid you in visualizing the completed puzzle. On "One Million Dollar Chance of a Lifetime" you are able to view all the letters that fit into the puzzle beforehand. On '"Scrabble" you are only permitted to see two letters at a time; and on "Wheel of Fortune" you will randomly pick consonants and vowels out of the entire alphabet.

The most frequently used vowels are *e* and *a*. If you have to

Contestant Testimonial

CHRISTY NEMETZ, 14 years old, Los Angeles, California

"It's hard for me to remember what happened those two days I won on 'Wheel of Fortune.' Everything was such a blur because there was so much excitement!

"I had watched 'Wheel of Fortune' all my life . . . well, for at least three years. I tried out for a Teen Week they were having and ended up getting on. I met Pat and Vanna. Vanna's sooooo skinny! But I had a feeling that I would win. I told myself 'Christy, you're going to win!' You see, I'm good with letters and phrases. They come easy for me. And I think they chose me because I've got a good outlook on life—because I've got a lot of spirit. I played the other champions and won, so I became the big winner of the week.

"It was funny, I just kept guessing puzzle after puzzle. I remember my first puzzle, it was 'Make a Lasting Impression,' and my last one was 'Follow the Leader.' That was a hard one. It only had ___ ___ L L ___ ___ - T ___ E - L E ___ ___ E R *showing. I went through the entire alphabet in my mind and guessed it with only a half a second left.*

"I won $25,000, including a car, a trip to Tahiti, a $5,000 savings bond, two stereos, and all kinds of other prizes. I feel like I have really accomplished something good. I also feel real famous. I'm the big star in the neighborhood. Everybody wanted to borrow my VCR tape. Friends were calling me all day and night. I feel good knowing people at home watched me and said to themselves, 'If she can do it, I can do it too!' "

pick a consonant, begin with the most common ones: *s, l, t, n, r,* and *d*. If you have tried all the common consonants and vowels, go through the entire alphabet in your mind to help you figure out what that first letter might be. For example, if you saw a puzzle that read _ A _ A _ L E, you should mentally insert *A* as the first letter of the word, and think about all the possibilities; then try a *B*, then a *C*, and so on. When you tried the letter *C*, the solution probably became very clear. The word is *capable*.

If there is some type of punctuation mark included in the puzzle, use it. Hyphens, apostrophes, exclamation points, and accent marks can all be very helpful when trying to solve a puzzle. If the category is "Things," it's a good bet that the letter *s* will appear at the end of the word.

On some game shows, you earn extra points or money for each letter or word you guess that fits into the puzzle. Others will deduct money or points for each letter that fits. If you know the answer, don't waste time, money, or points or risk the game by playing on—solve it immediately! I've seen too many people get greedy and end up losing everything.

Celebrity guest Brian Mitchel gives visual and verbal clues to his partner on "$100,000 Pyramid"

For example, Michael Hensley admitted to getting a little cocky after winning $10,400 in three days on "Wheel of Fortune." He had enough money to buy the grandfather clock that his wife, Sue, had always wanted, but he decided to spin again so that he might win enough to buy a stereo for himself as well. He landed on "Lose a Turn" and never got the opportunity to buy the clock *or* the stereo. Michael now advises contestants to "quit while they're ahead!"

When attempting to solve a puzzle, avoid inserting words not commonly found in that particular phrase. If, for example, the actual expression is "skating on thin ice," don't say "skating on *very* thin ice." Conversely, don't forget to add the proper word to make the phrase complete. I lost my third game on "All Star Blitz" because I said, "Chip off the old block" instead of "*A* chip off the old block." My opponent had no idea of what the puzzle was before I attempted to solve it, but he quickly saw my error and capitalized on it.

COMMUNICATING WORDS

Your goal is to communicate clues to your partner as quickly and efficiently as possible. If after watching the show you are still unclear as to what you are allowed to do, either verbally or visually, don't hesitate to ask the coordinator.

"$25,000 Pyramid" will let you point to any part of your body and say, "This is my blank." You are also permitted to use any brand names in your clues (e.g., "Budweiser is a type of blank.") You may not rhyme words, but you may use various inflections, accents, and tones in your voice to illustrate "the opposite of" or other special hints when communicating a clue.

If during the "$25,000 Pyramid" bonus round your partner says, "open door," the category couldn't be "things that are opened," so it would have to be the opposite, "things that are closed." Another effective method is to have your partner fill in the missing word by using a sentence containing the word "blank" (e.g., "A blank in shining armor.") Be careful not to say the answer or any portion of it when giving your clue.

If you are tied up with your opponent's team on "$25,000 Pyramid" and are asked to choose a category beginning with a certain letter, select one that will help you sound out the word. If, for example, you have a choice of using words beginning with the letter *m* or the letter *c*, choose the *m* so that you can say the "mmmm" sound in your mind to get you thinking in the right direction. The letter *m* begins similar-sounding words such as "mother" or "mental," while the letter *c* begins many different sounding words such as "coffee" or "city," and it will make guessing more difficult for your teammate. Take advantage of odd letters like *k, j, o, x, q, z*. The words starting with these letters are so few that your teammate will have a better chance of guessing them all.

On "$25,000 Pyramid" you should always let the celebrity *give* the clues during the bonus round because that's all they practice doing before the game begins. If you ask them to receive, you'll be putting them under more pressure, which certainly won't increase your odds of winning.

When playing "Password," you may use only one descriptive word clue with no visual aids of any kind. You may use rhymes as well as different accents, tones, and inflections in your voice to help your partner guess the proper word. If, for example, your partner says the word "hot" with an obvious voice inflection, you should immediately think of the word "cold." If you want to tell your partner that there is a word that usually follows your clue, verbally drag out the end of that word. If, for instance, you wanted your partner to say the word "sea" and the best clue "ocean" had already been given but with no results, you could say "Redddd . . ." as if to indicate that something familiar should follow.

If you have to break the word into syllables to get your partner to guess it, do so quickly and efficiently. For example, if the word is "pancake" and you have already given the most definitive clues "flapjack" and "waffle" but your partner still didn't guess it, divide the word into syllables and say "pot," and if they guess correctly, "Birthdayyyy . . ."

When playing games like "Family Feud" or "Match Game," listen carefully to the question because there is usually a key word or phrase that will trigger the most logical response. Although there is no "wrong" answer, try to keep your answer current. Gene Rayburn from "Match Game" gave me the phrase "Incredible blank." I thought of many things, including "The Incredible Shrinking Man," but luckily I went with my first instincts and said "Incredible Hulk." Debra Sue Scott of "Mary Hartman, Mary Hartman" fame matched me and I won $5,000. She told everyone that she was thinking of saying "The Incredible Shrinking Man," but didn't because it was such an old movie that I might not remember it.

GUESSING

There are pros and cons to guessing answers. You only want to guess if you are in the right position to do so. Let's say, for example, that you have won the first round, but you need two out of three rounds to win the game. You are now in a good position to guess as you have a safe, comfortable lead. If you are wrong, the worst thing that could happen is that your opponent could tie you, which would result in a play-off game.

Should you attempt to guess an answer if the score is even or if you are losing? That all depends on how sure you are of your guess. Some guesses are total speculation, some are "gut feeling," and some are in the back of your mind, but take a couple of seconds to think through. Only you can judge what to do with a question when you are not *completely* sure of the answer.

You will find that many knowledge and/or trivia questions consist of two parts, the first often being obscure and the second being easy. If you buzz in first, you could be getting a jump on your opponent. But if you are wrong, you could lose money or even lose the game. It's a gamble to guess after hearing only the first part of a question, but it could pay off.

On ''Child's Play'' I buzzed in after hearing only two quick clues—''small'' and ''green''—with the correct answer—''pea''—to win the round. Practicing different word-association games helped me win that game. If you only heard the first part of the following question, would you be able to answer it?: ''When you tell a little kid about the facts of life, most people relate it to . . .'' You probably have a good idea of the answer, but if you had waited for the second part of the question—''What two animals?''—one of your opponents probably would have buzzed in with the correct answer—''The birds and the bees''—before you. The trick is to listen closely to the question and try to pick up on any key phrases (in this case ''the facts of life'') that will act as clues. This special skill is what separates the winners from the losers.

''Joker's Wild'' contestant Sue Hensley of Cypress, California, was asked to name a musical march as part of her audio question. She hadn't the foggiest idea what type of march it was, but it sounded very military. She logically considered what a good name for a military march might be, and rather than saying ''I don't know,'' she decided to take a stab in the dark and guessed ''Washington March.'' It turned out to be the correct answer, and she won the game, $3,300, a trip to Hong Kong, a sailboat, and many other wonderful prizes. Sue's advice is: ''If you don't know the answer to a question, don't give up until you have considered all the possibilities.''

If you are playing a game like ''Card Sharks,'' be sure to pay close attention to the cards that have already been revealed. If you have seen a 2, 8, 6, 4, and 3, and you have to decide whether the next card after a 7 is higher or lower, you might want to guess ''higher'' since you have already seen so many low cards. Usually, though, you should divide the deck in half and guess higher for an 8 or below and lower for a 9 and above. If you have an option to freeze on any card, do it on 7s, 8s, and 9s. These are dangerous middle-of-the-deck cards, and your odds will be close to 50 percent if you go either way.

If a show like ''Family Feud'' or ''Card Sharks'' asks you how many people out of a certain number would do something, don't think of what you would do but rather what you think the *majority* of people would do. While on "Card Sharks" I was asked, "Out of one hundred women surveyed, how many said they would take their bathing suit top off at a nude beach?" The only thing I knew for sure was that *I* wouldn't do it; therefore, I responded with a very low figure. My opponent said the number was higher, which was correct. I lost that round because I imposed my own standards and morals on the answer.

If you are on a show like "Hollywood Squares" or "All Star Blitz," where you must agree or disagree with a celebrity's answer, take into account the following:

1. Is it a personally relevant question? (e.g., a music question directed to Dolly Parton or a theater question asked of Charles Nelson Reilly.) If it is, you should trust the celebrities' judgment, for it is in their field of expertise.
2. If the celebrities have been correct with most of their answers, go ahead and agree with them; they will rarely try to bluff. If you come across a celebrity who doesn't seem to have much on the ball, use your best judgment to answer the question. Avoid calling on them unless you are forced to block your opponent.
3. Do the celebrities look unsure? If they become fidgety or hesitant, their body language is telling you they aren't sure of the answer. If they look as if they are just guessing, use your own instincts to answer the question.
4. Is the question unusual? Outlandish statements make the show more interesting, and they are usually true rather than false.

PASSING

Pass a question, puzzle, word, or card to your opponent only when it's clear that he or she has a better chance of losing than you do of winning. Be aware that passing can still be dangerous even when it's obvious that the surest way to beat the odds is to let your opponent take the risk. There is always the possibility that your opponent will know the subject matter better than you do or will be lucky enough to receive an easy question, puzzle, or card. Passing primarily involves luck, an element that is very difficult to control.

If you were playing on old shows such as "Press Your Luck" or "Strike It Rich," you might have passed your turn over to your opponent because you suspected that a treacherous "whammy" or "burglar" might appear on the screen, instantly eliminating you from the round or even the game. If you are on "Card Sharks" and have a dangerous middle-of-the-deck 7, with two unrevealed cards to go, it certainly would behoove you to let your competitor try to guess whether his or her remaining four cards are higher or lower. If you are the big winner on "The Price Is Right," you would pass the first showcase to your opponent if you aren't sure what to bid for it. You would only pass a word on "Password" if you felt your partner needed at least two clues before he or she could guess it correctly.

If you're playing a game against a time clock and have absolutely no idea of the answer, don't waste precious time dwelling on it. Pass it and move on to the next clue. If time and rules permit, you will be given the opportunity to go back to it. Getting stuck on one clue for too long can cost you money and even the game.

When you're in a situation in which you logically should pass your turn over to your opponent but you're on such a roll that you feel you should keep playing, follow your instincts and go with the flow. Positive self-vibrations are very important when playing a game, so try not to interrupt your winning streak. If you are "hot," play on and don't look back.

BLOCKING

You should always try to be the aggressor in the game. If it's a tick-tack-toe game like "Hollywood Squares," begin in the center square so that you will have four directions in which to move. Choosing one of the four corners is a good alternative because it opens up three possible rows for you to take.

Only when your opponent has the lead should you consider playing defensively and start blocking. When playing "Blockbusters" or "Hollywood Squares," keep in mind all the different ways your opponent could win so that you will know where to block first. When you do, be careful! Sometimes an incorrect answer from you will give your opponent the block and quite possibly the game.

BETTING

The strategies surrounding betting differ from game to game. If your opponent's score is higher, you must bet at least enough to tie him or her. If your scores are close, try to leave some cash or points in your account so that if your opponent misses the question after betting everything, you will end up the winner. And, if your competitor wins, you may still be able to walk away with some cash.

Even when you know the subject matter well, avoid betting a lot of money if your score is more than double that of your opponent(s). I've seen obvious winners-to-be get greedy, bet it all, and lose.

When given an unfamiliar category, bad playing card, or tough-looking puzzle, don't "bet the house." Play conservatively and you'll have a better chance.

AVOIDING PROBLEMS DURING TAPING

What should you do if you answer a question correctly and you aren't given credit for it? Or what if you know you pressed the buzzer before your opponent but it didn't go off right away? If you have *any* questions, or if you are having any problems with your equipment (buzzer, microphone, etc.), *wait* until the commercial break to bring them to the attention of the producer. *Never* contradict the host while the show is being taped. Everything can and will be taken care of later.

The Game Must Go On!

It was a big moment for a certain female contestant on the early game show "3 on a Match." She was about to be asked a question that could win her the game, a cash bonus, and a pile of fabulous prizes. Just as host Bill Cullen began reading the question, the contestant excitedly asked to be excused for a "nature break." Bill, realizing that a break at that time would cost the producer a lot of money replied, "The viewers at home wait for the commercial, perhaps you can go at the same time as them!"

The anxious contestant managed to "hold it in" throughout Bill's question, her own correct answer, and a rather lengthy description of all the prizes she had won. She then immediately turned to Bill and exclaimed, "Gee, thanks a lot, but can I go to the bathroom now?"

There might be times when you think you punched in first and want to go ahead and answer the question. This isn't a good idea because, as a contestant, you are not always in the best position to know if you *were* first. Wait for the host to acknowledge you. It is his job to lead the game.

If the host says that you have answered a question incorrectly and you disagree, wait until the break to ask the judges to check your answer. If you still feel that your answer was correct, despite what the judges said, check a reliable source for proof after the taping. If you are right, call the producer *immediately*. He or she will want to remedy the situation as soon as possible and avoid having hundreds of viewers writing letters to bring the error to his or her attention.

You will occasionally notice hosts introducing contestants from previous shows because the judges made an error. These things happen from time to time, and all game shows are very good about giving the contestant the benefit of the doubt along with the opportunity to play a new and fair game.

HANDLING THE EXCITEMENT OF WINNING

It's hard to explain to someone the feeling of winning on a TV game show, but it has got to be one of the greatest sensations in the world! Buzzers sound, lights flash, and the audience goes absolutely crazy. Backstage is a barrage of hugging, handshaking, back-slapping, and kissing. You're a winner! A champion! You believed in yourself and *you* made it happen!

I could not stop laughing when we were told on "Match Game" to get really excited if we won. If you had just won $5,000, would someone have to *tell* you to get excited? I don't think so. But believe it or not, there are some dos and don'ts regarding how you should handle yourself when you win.

A "Crosswits" contestant jumps for joy over his win

Many hosts have been injured by overly enthusiastic winners. Before taping "Child's Play," we were told that if we won we were only to shake host Bill Cullen's hand because he loses his balance easily.

Monty Hall, host of "Let's Make a Deal," had so many overly zealous participants on his show that after several years he made all the contestants leave their heavy signs and costume accessories behind when they played. So be careful if you decide to hug a host. A quick kiss on the cheek, however, will be permitted on most game shows.

You may jump up and down when you win, but be warned: the elevated wooden stage could collapse from too much pressure. Jumping could also prove embarrassing. A "Price Is Right" contestant once got so excited that her halter top fell to her waist—a prime example of the importance of a little self-composure!

After winning the game, it may be difficult to concentrate on what the host says you have won. When I won the bonus round on "All Star Blitz," I became so deliriously happy, I didn't pay attention to what the prize was. Not wanting to interrupt all the excitement, I waited until the taping break to ask the coordinator what it was that I had won. He told me it was a thirteen-piece signed lithograph suite by Salvador Dali, valued at $4,000. He then laughingly explained that it was no wonder I didn't hear what prize I had won, as the audience was cheering so loudly.

Everyone loves to see a student who is working his or her way through college earn a lot of cash on a game show. We rejoice, too, when a single mother of three children wins a houseful of furniture. But what if you win a prize that you don't want or need? Don't huff and puff—just smile graciously. Even if you have three cars in your garage, you should try to appear thrilled with having won one more. There are millions of people without transportation who rooted for you from their living rooms, so the least you can do is pretend you really appreciate your prize. If you don't have anything nice to say about that prize, refrain from saying anything.

After winning on "Child's Play" I was told I would receive (among many other things) a year's supply of Chinese noodles. Well, I love Chinese food, but an entire year's worth just boggled my mind. Nevertheless, I smiled in appreciation and later shared all those noodles with family and friends. There are a lot of things you can do with any prize, so don't let on that you are disappointed. You'll look like a real ingrate.

If you're the winner at the end of a show or in the middle of a game when the time is up, the host will ask you if you can come back tomorrow. Of course you can! Since anywhere from two to six shows are taped in a day, all you really need to do is change your outfit so it *appears* as if you've come back the next day. (Ah, the magic of TV!)

Beth Fiance, "Scrabble" contestant coordinator, adds this tip: "Don't walk away after you think the game has ended because

A Slip of the Hand

It was on "The Dating Game" that famous stripper Gypsy Rose Lee chose Bachelor Number Two, a good-looking, Nordic gentleman, to be her date. The crowd seemed genuinely pleased with her selection, and they roared with approval.

The bachelor smiled and guided his arm around Gypsy's waist. But in all the excitement, his hand inadvertently touched her breast. Furious, Gypsy hauled off and whacked him right across the kisser. The cameraman kept his lens focused on the bachelor's face, despite the fact that blood had started trickling down from his nose. The brave bachelor continued to smile as the couple was told that their dream date would be a trip to Russia.

Gypsy called the producer years later to tell him that she and Bachelor Number Two were still dating and had a wonderful relationship. When the producer reminded Gypsy of the incident, she replied, "Well, I had to protect my virtue, didn't I?"

usually the camera is still rolling. Stay put until you are given a cue that it's time for you to walk off stage."

You will have about fifteen to twenty minutes to be escorted back into the holding room and change your outfit. Don't worry about changing your hair style or makeup. The makeup artist will be on the set to touch you up if you need it. If you have forgotten your stockings, shoes, tie, or anything else for that matter, the coordinator will almost always be able to help. He or she will also make sure you and your opponent are color coordinated so you look great standing next to each other.

Whether you have won $100,000 or just consolation prizes, you will be given a form to sign immediately after you have played. This document lists the delivery date, fabric, style, color, and size of all the prizes you have won. Read it carefully, and make sure you receive a copy for your records.

After your taping, you will no doubt be emotionally and physically exhausted. Seeing your friends and family will be your first priority, but you won't be allowed to go into the audience, and they won't be permitted backstage. You will have to share your victory with them outside the studio.

Before you leave, be sure to ask the coordinator when your show will air. If you have friends or family living out of town who want to catch you on TV, ask for the air date for their area(s) too.

LOSING

Unfortunately, along with the thrill of victory there will *always* be the agony of defeat. If you do everything you humanly can, but your opponent is just a faster or better player, or if you become too tired to concentrate, pat yourself on the back anyway. It takes a lot of skill and confidence to make it through the interviews, the glaring hot lights, the obtrusive cameras, and the pressure of answering questions literally within seconds.

It's easy for friends and family to brag about how *they* would do, but you don't see them competing on TV, do you? Not everyone has that much courage, so be proud of yourself. And

"Joker's Wild" Host Jack Barry congratulates an obviously pleased champion

remember, you won't walk away empty-handed; you will be awarded parting gifts worth up to $1,000 for your hard work.

Whether you win or lose on a game show, you will have an "in" for getting on any future shows or pilots you might wish to try out for (see chapter 8). Cary and Cathy Schorr won thousands of dollars in cash and prizes on "Match Game," "Wheel of Fortune," and "Chance of a Lifetime." Cathy told me, "I know we were chosen to film those shows because of our first experience on 'The Newlywed Game.' Contestant coordinators look at you better and longer than the other new players. Once you do a game show, it's almost like having a résumé!"

Chapter 5

Attitude: Playing to Win

When it comes to game shows and contests, there will always be people who say things like, "She was just lucky," or "If only I had some luck, I would have won." Make no mistake, a little luck can go a long way. But to be a winner, you really have to think like a winner. The best way I can teach the philosophy of winning is to illustrate how quickly you lose when you *don't* have it. And lose is precisely what I did on my first game show.

I had always considered myself lucky. I had won raffles, poker tournaments, and other small contests. So when I decided to try out for a game show, I naturally expected to do well. I soon learned never to take winning for granted. My happy-go-lucky attitude got me through a 300-applicant interview for my first game show in 1980. The game was "Card Sharks," and the host was Jim Perry.

I arrived early on my taping day and entered the large studio proudly displaying my five changes of wardrobe, in case I should win five straight games. The sight of the equipment, crew, and other contestants made me a bit nervous, but as soon as the coordinator isolated us in a special briefing room, I began to loosen up. She explained the rules, and we played a few short mock games. We were told that the taping would begin in a few hours, so we took the opportunity to get to know one another better. It was during this period of time that my troubles began.

I was told by several other contestants who had returned from the week before that out of the thirty people in the room, twenty-five were returnees, many back for the fifth and sixth time. It seemed quite clear that I would never be chosen to play that day since it was my first time in the studio. I believed what the other players-to-be told me. I began to think that it would actually be better to come back because next time I would know what to expect.

Some of the contestants were very concerned with who among them would be chosen to play next, but I stopped worrying and just started enjoying myself. A couple of "pros" told tales of past game show adventures, and everyone seemed in great spirits.

The taping was delayed for another hour. I played card games with a few of the other contestants. Someone had brought along a radio, and a couple of us even started dancing! I was having a sensational time, and then the bomb dropped.

The red "hotline" phone sitting in the corner of the room suddenly started ringing. The coordinator picked it up. Someone informed me that it was the producer at the other end telling the coordinator which contestant he wanted to play next. I smiled and continued chatting. I wasn't the least bit concerned since I really believed I would have to come back the next week. Then I felt a tap on my shoulder. "Congratulations, Marla! You've been chosen to play last week's champion," hollered the coordinator.

My heart sank into my stomach. I couldn't catch my breath for what seemed like hours. "But there has to be some mistake," I mumbled faintly. "No mistake," replied the coordinator. "The producer wants *you,* so let's go!"

Twenty-nine sets of eyes glared at me. The people who had been so nice were suddenly disgruntled. And for good reason—they had come back week after week hoping to play, and I was merely a "first-timer." I began to plead with the coordinator to pick somebody else. When the group sensed the fear and dread I was feeling, they instantly came to my rescue. They stood up and started shouting, "Come on, Marla, you can do it!"

The thought of having to play a two-time returning champion made me feel I might actually suffer a heart attack (and mind you, I was only twenty-four at the time!). I had to tell the coordinator I was going to be sick. She said, "You're just a little nervous." Well, she was wrong. I wasn't nervous—I was terrified!

She guided me out of the contestant's room and onto the stage. Then she whispered to the host about my "slight apprehension." My knees were knocking when the host, Jim Perry, came over. He was very comforting. He told me not to worry and to try and have fun. He did make me feel better, and I ended up doing well during my introduction, despite the fact that I didn't want to be there in the first place.

Then Jim introduced the champ, and my new-found confidence took a nose dive. When she stood next to me, I felt both physically and mentally bowled over. Her "high-energy presence" was so evident that if I could have bottled it, I would have made a fortune!

The reality of the situation became crystal clear—she wanted to win and I wanted to get off the stage. I didn't think about my family and friends in the audience. I didn't think about how lucky I usually am. I didn't try to have fun. Instead, I focused on the negative: "The champ is better than I am. I am not ready to play. Let me lose so I can get out of here!"

Needless to say, I was beaten badly and very quickly. But I was never the same after that frightening experience. From that moment on, I decided to learn from my mistakes and change my entire strategy for my future game shows. I wanted to play and to win, and I was never going to let myself be psyched out again!

Bob Barker reveals a stage filled with fabulous prizes to a very surprised "The Price Is Right" winner

I went on to play on three shows after that—"Match Game," "Child's Play," and "All Star Blitz." I won more than $20,000 in cash and prizes, and I had a great time doing it. Here is my formula for winning:

BELIEVE IN YOURSELF

In order to win, you must believe that you can. All individuals form ideas about themselves early on, and those basic beliefs eventually determine what they become. We cannot be or do more than we believe we can.

We have the power to think whatever we choose. If something pops into our head, we have the power to make it go away, even if we don't know why we chose to think it in the first place. You have strong powers within yourself that you are capable of stimulating when you choose. You must acknowledge the fact that you control your own mental world. If you aren't convinced, answer this question: If you don't control your thoughts, who does? Is it your boss? Your mother? Your spouse? No, it's you and you alone.

If you are determined to improve yourself, you must be in control of your mind instead of letting your mind control you. It may require strict discipline to train your mind to think in this new creative pattern, but nothing worthwhile is easy.

The amazing untapped power we have within us is of a force and quality that most of us cannot fully comprehend. We tend to underrate ourselves. To counteract the crippling effect of such self-criticism, practice thinking optimistically about your own possibilities. Once you stop focusing on your limitations and become excited about your potential, new qualities will appear within you. You will be able to do and be what formerly seemed impossible.

I'll never forget a story an old friend of mine told me about a World Series baseball game that took place many, many years ago between the New York Yankees and the Chicago White Sox. In the fifth inning the score was 4 to 3, Chicago. Babe Ruth had hit a home run in the first inning, but the Chicago pitcher didn't seem worried that he might do it again.

Babe swung and missed. Strike one! The second ball came whizzing across. Strike two! Everyone in the stands that day started to wonder if he would actually strike out at that crucial point in the game. Then Ruth did a very strange thing. He raised his finger, smiled, and pointed straight across the fence as if to indicate where he intended to hit the ball. The pitch came, and the Babe sent that ball flying right across the fence he had pointed to.

After the game a reporter asked Babe Ruth, "What if you had missed the final pitch?" Babe, with a genuine look of surprise, answered, "Why, I never even thought of such a thing!"

The best way for you to absorb this approach to life fully is to practice the strength of belief even before you try out to become a game show contestant. Obstacles or difficult tasks (like passing the interview) need never defeat you. As Ralph Waldo Emerson once said, "No accomplishments, no assistance, no training can compensate for lack of belief." Accept that as a fact. Hold confidence firmly in your mind until it becomes a reality, and you will have made a great achievement.

When Lisa and Dan Smith drove their old, broken-down car from Rhode Island to Hollywood and moved into an unfurnished apartment, they knew things *had* to get better. Once settled in, Lisa and Dan began discussing their ambitions and dreams, one of which was getting to play on "The Price Is Right" and meeting host Bob Barker.

Two months later they found themselves in the studio with Contestant Coordinator Johnny Olsen telling Lisa to "Come on down!" When Bob Barker revealed a beautiful new car behind the curtain, Lisa knew it was "meant to be." Even though she had not practiced pricing different kinds of merchandise, the thought of losing never entered her mind.

With her mother-in-law and husband, Dan, in the audience giving her critical moral support, Lisa went on to win $26,000 in prizes, including a car, a ski boat, a trip to New Orleans, five bars of gold, a sixty-three-piece china set, and a gold watch. Lisa simply couldn't imagine herself losing—and she didn't!

Lisa Smith's victory illustrates that *big faith equals big results!* This is the formula by which big things are done and by which big difficulties are overcome. I use this formula not just for game shows but for all aspects of my life, and you can too! If you want to win, you must first believe in yourself. Once you have mastered that, you can continue to develop the winning edge by keeping a positive mental attitude.

KEEP A POSITIVE MENTAL ATTITUDE

"Child's Play" contestant Lisa Mills from Los Angeles, California, used what she calls a "Rocky attitude." She kept the "Eye of the Tiger'' approach in mind throughout her taping. Being positive and feeling ''real up'' helped her to concentrate on the questions asked. She played for five days in a row, winning $13,500 in cash!

If I had believed in myself back in 1980, I could easily have attained a positive mental attitude on the ''Card Sharks'' set. I could think up all kinds of lame excuses for why I didn't win. I could say that I wasn't prepared to play that day because of what the other contestants had told me. I could moan about it being my first game show and about the fact that I didn't know what to expect. But I have only myself to blame, for through the entire experience, I only saw the negative.

Never say things to yourself like, ''I'll look stupid if I don't win and my friends will be ashamed of me'' or ''I'm not smart enough to win.'' I think Mark Twain captured our insecurities when he said, ''We are all ignorant . . . just about different things!'' When you think you are stupid, you are acting from fear and not from strength. Fear is supported by all the thoughts we use to avoid dealing with it directly. You will never know how wonderful it feels to rid yourself of a fear until you risk doing something you're afraid of.

Speaking before a group of people is scary. There is no way to guarantee that everything will turn out well when you're on camera. If a guarantee were necessary, there wouldn't be anyone brave enough to be on television. The future is promised to no one.

If you give the wrong answer, nobody is going to hang you upside-down by your toenails. You are playing the game to have fun, regardless of the outcome.

Most contestants are friendly and good-natured, but a couple in each crowd are usually openly competitive. Don't let these people who have worked themselves up into a frenzy frighten you. When Rhonda Stone played on ''Family Feud,'' she came away with some wonderful memories. Unfortunately, her ''Wheel of Fortune'' experience wasn't as pleasant. During the taping break, one of her opponents bitterly told her, ''You better not win anymore!'' She didn't reply, but when it came time to play again, she was more determined than ever to win. She didn't let her opponent's threats and negativity get to her. Instead, she forged ahead to win the game and $4,000 in prizes! Negative, hostile, or obnoxiously competitive players, usually don't win because their underlying insecurities distract them. Their mental slant is tinged with thoughts of failure, so naturally they fail.

The same is true of worrying. You will become slow and even inept at playing the game if you don't control your worries. Once they have gotten hold of you, you can kiss all the money and prizes good-bye! The secret to overcoming worry is to substitute faith and positive feelings for fear. If a rude contestant says something to you like, "You'll never be chosen" or "If I play you, I am going to win," stay cool, calm, and above all, *positive*. Walk away and continue feeling good about yourself. Leave them to their own "head trips." Don't debate, lecture, or waste valuable time and energy trying to change them.

A player may use the old pity ploy on you as well, even unintentionally. It goes something like this: "Looks as though we'll be playing each other. I just wanted you to know that my kid is real sick and I sure could use the money to pay the bills," or "I've never won anything in my life and I'll probably lose today." If you are feeling confident enough, go ahead and give these people a shot of "good will." Tell them to think positively. My philosophy is, when you help someone else, you'll probably feel better about yourself.

In fact, being positive about others is part of being positive about yourself. Be glad when others win, and celebrate with them. Never compare yourself or your achievements with others; make comparisons only with your own goals. This will often make your standards much higher.

Stacey Brower from Fayetteville, Arkansas, won more than $12,000 in cash and prizes on "The Price Is Right." She shared with me her experience of being selected out of an audience of 400 people: "Even though I had to wait four hours in line, I made a lot of friends—people from all over. I was having so much fun, I didn't care if I was picked. It was so exciting seeing Bob Barker! But inside I felt like I was going to

Every day is a joyous Halloween on "Let's Make a Deal"

be chosen anyway. I kind of talked myself into it. I even told everyone in line that I was going to be on the show. I figured that, because I am a positive thinker, and basically a good person, I deserved it!''

Stacey's positive attitude and strong believe in herself made it possible for her to win. Don't let yourself be a victim of self-imposed limitations. Even if your ability and experience are less than other peoples', you can compensate for almost anything with enthusiasm.

USE CREATIVE VISUALIZATION

Now that you're feeling confident and positive, use guided imagery to help you gear up for playing and winning the game. Start by getting into a very comfortable, relaxed position and painting a mental picture of the events on your taping day.

Visualize yourself playing the game, talking confidently with the host, solving puzzles, and answering questions quickly and easily. Imagine yourself having fun and winning money and great prizes. Actors, athletes, and many others use this visualization technique to enhance their performance.

While Steve and Connie Rutenbar were waiting to play "One Million Dollar Chance of a Lifetime," they noticed that some of the couples seemed quite friendly but others just kept to themselves. The Rutenbars decided to spend some time getting to know people and then make time to be alone so that they could prepare for the game by visualizing themselves playing and winning. This strategy definitely helped, for the Rutenbars went on to achieve the honor of being the first couple to win the million dollars!

Even if you are equipped with strong self-confidence, a positive mental attitude, and a solid understanding of the game, you may not feel secure without your good-luck piece. If that's the case, go right ahead and bring it along! I've seen people hang on to all kinds of unusual lucky charms; everything from locks of hair to large stuffed animals. These pieces symbolize faith and hope—things we can always use more of. Feel free to mention your good-luck trinket to the host too. It will make a great conversation piece for your introduction.

In summary, if you want to play to win, you must believe in yourself! Think positive and visualize success! If you do, you will set in motion a powerful force that will help you tackle anything that crosses your path. When I held a winning mental attitude for the three games I played after "Card Sharks," I was actually able to control the course of the games.

8 STEPS FOR GAINING CONTROL

You're on stage standing next to the champion, and your mind is racing in a thousand different directions. This is a very important time for you to take control. You can accomplish this in eight easy steps:

1. Use the first few minutes on stage to get yourself adjusted to the lights, cables, cameras, and your own body placement. Take some deep breaths. Concentrate on your breathing. This will slow down your rapidly beating heart and calm your nerves.
2. Practice quietness within your mind and body. You can alleviate mental and muscular tension by just saying to yourself, "Be still nerves, be still heart." You will then feel the tension leaving your body. Use your mind, not your emotions, to do this. Draw on the inner source of power found deep within you. One of the best things about peace of mind is that it increases your intellectual power.
3. Surround yourself with a strong energy force. This may sound like something out of *Star Wars*, but the truth is, everyone possesses a certain amount of inner power or energy. The key is knowing how to make it work for you. To summon this inner source of strength, visualize a clear, white light, a positive energy force totally enveloping you. This force will shield you from all negative distractions. Your opponent will sense your powerful aura but will be unable to penetrate it.
4. Keep repeating, "I am going to win" in your mind. Only desperate players tell themselves, "I *need* to win" or "I *must* win." By focusing on the positive, you will give negative thoughts no opportunity to enter.

Some people like to set a goal for exactly how much they want to win. Though I won an average of $7,000 per game, I set my sights on winning only $5,000. I used that figure as a minimum goal; if I won more, it would be gravy. Barbara Schnell wanted to win $10,000 on the "$25,000 Pyramid" so that she could buy a new furnace for her home. She ended up winning $58,950 in cash, a trip to Jamaica, a VCR, and a home computer. If you want to set a figure in your mind, go ahead. If not, the sky's the limit!

5. Smile! This will serve as your reminder to have fun while playing the game. You also have a very special secret—you *know* you're going to win.
6. Concentration is one of the most important keys to playing and winning. Don't let anyone or anything distract you from solving the puzzle or answering the question. Put the stage, crew, lights and, most important, the cameras out of your mind. Pretend they don't exist. Once the game starts, most people forget they're in a studio, on camera, in front of millions of viewers. It becomes just you and the host. It almost feels as if you're playing the game in your own living room.

   Joy Wolpert, producer of "The Price Is Right," "Double Dare," "Phew!," and "Hitman," advises, "Keep your head! Quiet yourself to the question and only the question."

   Angela Grace and Mark Fogarty felt they blew the chance to win a million dollars on "One Million Dollar Chance of a Lifetime" because they both lost their concentration. Mark became distracted by the time clock ticking away, and then Angela became confused by Mark's distraction. They both let the pressure get to them.

   Michael Hensley was chosen as a contestant on "Hollywood Squares" soon after his wife, Sue, had been on and lost. She had found it difficult to decide which square to go to next because she was too busy listening to her opponent's questions and answers. The fact that the celebrities were seated so far away also contributed to her distraction.

   Michael learned a lot from his wife's experiences, and when he played the game, he dismissed all the cameras from his mind, as well as his opponent's questions. He concentrated on which celebrity he would call on next. His strategy worked, and he went on to win $8,000 in cash and prizes.

My friend Larry Goss, who won more than $25,000 in cash and prizes on "All Star Blitz," told me he concentrated only on himself, not on the strengths or weaknesses of his opponents. Make a point of blocking out any distractions, be it the cameras, the time clock, your nerves rattling, or the coffee stain on your sleeve. Focus only on your questions and where you will be moving to next.

7. Listen carefully to all questions. If you do not understand or miss part of the question, speak up and ask the host to repeat it. He will always be happy to oblige.

When "Match Game" host Gene Rayburn gave me

A "Hollywood Squares" contestant wins a new car with the help of a few celebrity players

the $5,000 bonus phrase ''Praying blank,'' I wasn't sure that I heard it correctly. I asked him to say it again, and not only did he repeat it, but he showed me the way it was spelled on his note card.

Seven-thousand-dollar ''Card Shark'' winner Martin Gold found it very difficult to concentrate on the questions asked after his third day because he was so tired from the excitement of winning the previous games. He didn't listen closely to the question ''Out of one hun-

Contestant Testimonial

KISS AND TELL

TAMMY EISELE, Anaheim Hills, California

''Game shows are the greatest! When I moved out from Florida to California, I opened a flower and gift shop with my friend Diane. One day, out of nowhere, the contestant coordinator for 'All Star Blitz' came up to Diane and asked her if she wanted to try out for the show. Like any good friend, Diane asked if I could interview too. We both went to the interview and both passed. It was such a fluke!

''I never thought about the cameras, the producer, or the staff; I just got totally involved in the game. The first puzzle I guessed in the bonus round was ''A Joint Venture.'' It was quite appropriate because of my partnership with Diane. Everything happened so quickly then. I won that first game, then the second game, and before I knew it, I had played for five straight days.

''When Peter Marshall told me I had won $22,400 in cash and prizes, I was blown away. I just couldn't stop kissing him—I was so excited! The producer had to holler 'Cut' because Peter had my lipstick all over his face and they needed to clean him up. Peter didn't seem to mind. I guess it's just all in a day's work for a game show host.''

dred dentists, how many admitted they had pulled the wrong tooth?'' and it did him in. He missed the word ''admitted'' in the question, so he guessed a high figure. His opponent named a lower figure which was correct, since only twelve dentists actually *admitted* they had ever pulled the wrong tooth. As Martin's experience demonstrates, if you hesitate to ask the host to repeat a question, it could be your last.

8. Don't let taping breaks or technical delays interfere with the flow of your game. Instead, use those breaks to your advantage. If you're in the middle of the game and the host interrupts to announce a commercial, take those few minutes to practice the playing-to-win techniques you've learned. As the game progresses, you will become more relaxed, more confident, and more eager to win.

Jim Lange of ''Dating Game'' fame, now host of ''One Million Dollar Chance of a Lifetime,'' told me a story that happened when he was the host for ''Name That Tune.'' A female contestant guessed the song's title—''I Feel Like I Am Falling''—and right after she said it, she somehow lost her balance and fell over. The producer called for a quick break. They picked her up and made sure she was okay. When taping began again, Jim quickly eased her embarrassment by saying, ''You don't have to show me the title, you just have to tell me!'' She laughed, regained her composure, and then immediately refocused her attention on the game.

I will never forget what happened while I was playing the ''Child's Play'' bonus round. I was in the middle of guessing word clues under a thirty-second time clock when suddenly the producer yelled, ''Cut.'' Apparently, one of the technicians backstage misheard me and gave me credit for a wrong answer. I was told I had a choice of either continuing with the thirteen seconds I had left on the clock or starting a new bonus round. I wasn't sure what to do.

The host, Bill Cullen, looked at the new set of word clues and said, ''Marla, start a new game. These clues look easy. I'm sure you will guess all of them.'' I asked for a new game and before it started, I closed my eyes and told myself repeatedly, ''You can do this, just concentrate!'' Thanks to Bill Cullen's confident advice and my refocused concentration, I won that $5,000 bonus!

Chapter 6

Preparation: Your Taping Day

Now that you have watched, studied, and practiced your game as much as you possibly can, your playing strategies are crystal clear, you firmly believe you are capable of playing a good game, and you are ready to take control and concentrate on winning, your dream of being on a game show is about to become a reality. This will truly be one of the most exciting days of your life!

PREPARATION

When the coordinator gives you your taping date, time, and location, be sure to ask how long the taping could last, in case you have prior commitments that night or even the next day. You will not be allowed to make phone calls, so bear in mind that you will spend several hours at the studio, especially if any technical or mechanical delays occur. If you are from out of town and for some reason you are not chosen to play the first day, be prepared to stay another day or come back the following week.

Ask for detailed directions to the studio and arrive ten to fifteen minutes early, just as you did for your interview. You will be asked to come approximately three hours before the taping is due to begin. This time will be used to brief you on all the rules and regulations, test the equipment, rehearse you, gear up the audience, and so on.

You may not bring children to the studio, so be sure to arrange for a baby sitter in advance.

Phone all your family and friends announcing your star-to-be status and then get a good, sound sleep the night before your taping. I realize how difficult sleeping can be (especially with dreams of cash, shiny new cars, and luxurious vacations floating through your mind), but it's important that you try to get some sleep so that you'll be fresh and sharp for the game. If you have tried to sleep but the anticipation of the next day's events is keeping you awake, do what you would normally do for insomnia: take a long, hot shower or bath, have your back rubbed, or have a cup of warm milk, noncaffeine tea, or a glass of wine. Stay away from the sleeping pills as most varieties will leave you feeling drowsy the next day.

Regardless of whether you're hungry or not the day of your taping, eat a good-sized breakfast or lunch before going to the studio. This meal will help you keep your energy level up before the lunch or dinner break. It may even have to sustain you through the entire taping if you're too nervous to eat anything at the studio. (Believe it or not, I spent close to ten hours in the "Match Game" studio due to the various delays.)

When your taping day exceeds six hours, many shows will provide you with a lunch or dinner. You may even be invited to eat with the staff of the show—including any celebrity players. Unfortunately, however, you are not allowed to speak to them. This strict "no talking to anyone" policy ensures that contestants are not receiving help of any kind from the stars or any member of the staff.

The four shows I played on served delicious lunch and dinner buffets that included salads, fruits, soups, a wide variety of hot main dishes, juices, soft drinks, and many delectable desserts.

As fate would have it, I was too excited to enjoy most of those goodies.

One more tip: don't drink a lot of coffee. You'll be "hyper" enough anyway, and you won't have the opportunity to keep visiting the restroom.

What to Bring

You will be asked to bring some sort of identification with you (a driver's license is sufficient) and something with your Social Security number on it (an income tax return, pay stub, legal document, etc.,) but not a Social Security card, which cannot be used for identification. The coordinator will tell you exactly what his or her production company or network requires as proof that you are who you say you are.

It's also a good idea to bring along a portable game like backgammon or cards, or a knitting or needlepoint project, just in case there are a lot of delays. If you will be playing a knowledge game, take along a few reference books that you and the other contestants can use to quiz each other. Bring along your copy of *Be a TV Game Show Winner!* too. You can practice your game-playing techniques while waiting. Playing games or working with your hands will help pass the time and relieve the anticipation tension that you will feel after many hours of waiting. You will probably become friendly with the other contestants and they too will welcome the diversion and chance to practice before it is their turn to play.

What to Wear

Your coordinator will tell you how many different outfits to bring on your taping day and what type of clothing is acceptable. In order that you be seen clearly on TV, you may be told to stay away from colors used in the game's background. Tiny checks or dots, very narrow stripes, busy prints, shiny blouses, or corduroy can also cause problems for the camera. White blouses or shirts can "burn" through the camera and create a ghostlike image through subsequent camera shots. Black can be just as bad.

I prefer to wear lively, cheerful colors in hopes that the producer will pick me sooner to compete. Don't wear anything too dull, fluorescent, tight, or sexy. Women may be asked to wear dresses or skirts, and men may be asked to wear ties and jackets.

The studio is always cold when you first arrive, so bring along a sweater or jacket. Once the audience is seated and the taping begins, the hot lights will make the studio more comfortable.

Some people prefer to have their hair and makeup professionally done before appearing on television, but it certainly is not mandatory. If you pay to get all fixed up and they don't choose you to play that day, you're going to be very disappointed. So do your own hair and makeup at home, and if the producer deems it necessary, he will have his makeup artist touch up your hair and face.

AT THE STUDIO

When you arrive at the studio, nice and calm because you have made it with time to spare, a staff assistant will greet you at the entrance and escort you to the contestant holding room where you will be given a name tag to wear. This is for the host's convenience, since it can be hard for him to remember everyone's name.

This is an exhilarating time and a good chance to get to know the other contestants. You will find yourself becoming friendly with people even when you have to compete against them. The first day I was on "Child's Play," I became friendly with a young woman named Monica. I won two games in a row, and when I returned for the next day's taping, she was waiting for me with an armful of "good-luck" flowers. Her sweet gesture only enhanced my already positive state of mind.

Then the worst thing happened. The producer put Monica up *against* me, the returning champ. My conscience told me that I

A few "All Star Blitz" contestants waiting in the contestant holding room for their big chance to play (I am second from the left)

had won the crown long enough, so I decided to stifle my competitive spirit. The game began and, even though I knew the answers, I didn't buzz in immediately. Despite my efforts to give her every possible advantage, by a strange twist of fate, she answered all the questions incorrectly, which left me champion once again. I felt terrible about beating her, but luckily she never held a grudge and we are friends to this day.

Inviting Guests

You will be able to invite guests to the studio to watch your taping, but children under sixteen years of age will not be permitted. Family and friends can pick up their tickets under your name at the "will call," or box office, window approximately one hour before the taping is due to begin. Some shows

Did You Know That . . .

* One of "Dynasty's" biggest stars got her first American television exposure on a game show? The celebrity was Joan Collins, the game was "Password," and the year was 1963. Collins and her then-husband, Anthony Newley, were guest stars for a week on the "Password" set in New York. Years later, Ms. Collins was also on "Match Game," "Rhyme and Reason," "Crosswits," and countless other shows. She was considered a very fine player on the game show circuit.

* Boy George and his group, Culture Club, appeared on the only rock-and-roll game show, "The Pop 'n Rocker Game" in 1983? Culture Club was just starting to make some progress on the music charts with their first hit, "Do You Really Want to Hurt Me?" when they were offered the opportunity to appear on national television. George and friends sang live on the show, and the audience went wild.

* Game show creator and host Chuck Barris wrote a number-one best-selling book entitled *You and Me Babe*? Barris wrote the book in the early seventies while he was at the height of his game show success with both "The Dating Game" and "The Newlywed Game" in prime time, as well as daytime. Barris penned his first number-one hit in the late fifties, only that time it was a record—"Palisades Park," sung by Freddie Cannon.

allow as many as ten guests per contestant; others only five. If you do not request tickets for your guests in advance, none will be held for them.

I believe that having friends and family in the audience helps you play a better game. They give moral support and make the greatest cheering section you could ever find. Some contestants

Joan Collins, "Password" Host Allen Ludden, and Joan's then-new husband, Anthony Newley

disagree with me on this issue, however. They feel their family made them nervous and sometimes even distracted them. The choice of whether to have family or friends attend the taping is solely yours.

When my friend Dinah was on "Card Sharks," I arrived early, sat in the front row, and yelled out whether I thought she should guess "higher" or "lower." She definitely felt more confident seeing and hearing me in the audience. Some shows allow audience participation; others do not.

If you plan to invite guests to the taping, ask them to arrive early for a front-row seat. Let them know that there will be a long wait and that there is a possibility that they might be put into a "special" section of the audience where they will not have as good a view of you. This seating arrangement is used by some shows to ensure that your friends and family don't aid you in answering any of the questions.

Rules and Regulations

You are allowed to look briefly at your family and friends in the audience, but never wave, gesture, or talk to them.

Speaking to celebrity guests, staff personnel, or even just people milling around the studio can get you into a heap of trouble—not the least of which is your immediate dismissal from the show. Play it safe and only speak to the coordinator, producer, and other contestants. Since the game show scandal of 1958 when contestants were given answers to questions and puzzles (see chapter 10), producers don't want to take any chances. Production companies and networks are very, very careful with their contestants. They can't risk having their reputation smeared and their show canceled.

Although the Federal Communication Commission governs all the individual networks, every network has its own "watchdog" department that guards against game fixing. CBS refers to their department as Program Practices; NBC calls theirs Compliance & Practices; and ABC uses the title Broadcast Standards. Some stations have their representatives randomly select the questions, while others have them choose who will play and when. This prevents contestants from finding out which questions will be used for their game. Since the network is ultimately responsible for the integrity of the programs it airs, network representatives may also be in the studio, making sure no one discusses the questions and answers to be used on the show. You will be escorted everywhere, including to the bathroom, to ensure that this strict rule is enforced.

Release Forms

Before the taping begins, your coordinator will instruct you as to the rules and regulations, and you will have to sign a waiver or release form indicating that you have read and understood everything. Most general release forms cover the following:

1. You will abide by all the rules and regulations set out in the release, and if you fail to do so, you will be required to forfeit your appearance as well as any cash and/or prizes you might have won.
2. You or your family do not have an association with anyone connected with the game, its staff, agents, distributors, subsidiaries, or sponsors.
3. You are not and will not be a candidate for public office. (This is to guard against the opposing political party demanding equal time on the show.)
4. You are over eighteen years of age (unless, of course, you are playing on a special children or teen-week program).
5. You will be responsible for all travel risks and expenses connected with the game whether or not you are selected as a contestant.
6. You will not mention or "plug" your employer or school while on the air; nor will you accept money or gifts for talking about commercial products or services. If you do, you will be breaking a federal law that is punishable by a fine and/or a jail sentence.
7. If you are selected to play, the producer is under no obligation to broadcast your show or award you cash or prizes you might have won, if the show does not air.
8. You waive all perpetual media rights worldwide, and everything you do and say on the program will belong to the producer to do with as he pleases without additional compensation to you, other than those prizes you originally won on the program.
9. You agree to pay federal, state, and city taxes, including income, use, or sales tax, on all prizes you win.
10. You will notify the producer of any delay in receiving or damage to any prizes you have won. If the supplier

is unable to furnish the exact prizes described on the show, you will agree to accept a substitute prize of equal or greater value or the cash equivalent.

11. If you decide to sell any of your prizes, you will not use the show's name in the ad.

12. Any travel and/or lodging accommodations you win will not be transferred, exchanged, sold, or redeemed and will only be used by you at such time as specified by the producer or the supplier.

13. If a technical delay occurs, you will agree to abide by the producer's decision as to when the game may resume or whether the cash and/or prizes will be awarded.

14. You will not be a contestant if you have been on any game show in the last twelve months. You will list the names and dates of all the game shows on which you have appeared.

15. If you are a member of any performing arts union, you will list the name(s) of the union(s).

16. You will agree to release and indemnify all sponsors and broadcasters from all liability, claims, actions, damages, expenses, and losses caused by any statement you will have made in connection with your appearance on the show. (If, for example, you say something libelous about your employer, you would be held responsible, not the producer or sponsor.)

17. You were given ample opportunity to read the release and its rules and regulations and understand and agreed to be bound by each and every item contained therein.

If you have *any* questions regarding the release, ask the contestant coordinator about it before you sign. You should receive a copy of the release as soon as you have read and signed it.

Warming up

The next step in the taping process is called a ''warm-up'' or ''briefing.'' The coordinator will settle down those contestants who are exceptionally nervous and ''psyche up'' those who are a little too calm. Everyone should be a bit apprehensive, however, because we tend to react better under stress.

The playing rules will be explained again so that you will have a perfect understanding of the game. If you have any questions, this is the time to ask them. Some shows, like ''Let's Make a Deal'' or ''The Price Is Right,'' require little or no prior briefing for their participants. They select their contestants from the studio audience just before they tape or while they're actually on the air.

After all the speeches have been made, appropriate documents signed, and questions answered, you'll have some time to kill. Take advantage of this valuable time by practicing the playing-to-win exercises in chapter 5. These mental warm-ups are essential for competing and winning.

During this period you can also enjoy the light snacks and drinks that will be provided by most production companies.

If there are two or three of you wearing the same color clothing, the coordinator may ask one of you to change into an outfit with a contrasting color. You might also be asked to change if you clash or blend in too much with the set decor. If the producer feels you need a little hair or face touch-up, he or she will send you over to makeup at this time.

When I was on ''Match Game,'' I was sent over to makeup to get a coat of pancake and some eyeliner. In the chair next to me was John Davidson (currently the host of ''Hollywood Squares''). I started to say hello but was interrupted by the assistant coordinator, who reminded me that I was not allowed to speak to anyone except the makeup people. I can't tell you how much I wanted to talk with John, but I obeyed the rules and had fun just watching him get made up.

Sometime within this period you and the other contestants will be given the opportunity to see the actual set. When you

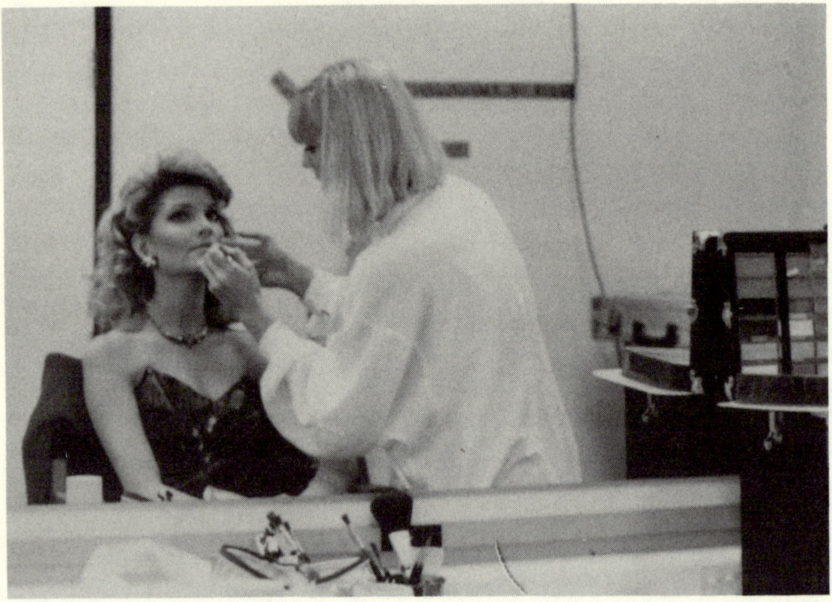

"One Million Dollar Chance of a Lifetime" Hostess Karen Thomas gets a quick facial touch up before taping begins

enter you will notice that the audience seating area is small—containing anywhere from 50 to 300 chairs—but when the camera focuses on the audience, it looks as though there are thousands of people. Another way the production company makes it appear as if there are more people in the audience is by amplifing the sounds of applause and cheering with a special machine during the actual taping. It may seem deceptive, but that's show biz.

The audience will not be seated inside the studio until the taping is about ready to begin, but the various technicians and stage personnel will be working around you. These technicians—video, audio, and lighting personnel—have been setting up since the wee hours of the morning. The production staff, director, and stage managers have distributed the scripts, the top-secret questions and answers, and the show's routine sheets showing what, when, where, and how everything will happen.

Even if there is no run-through, you will be shown where you should enter the stage as you go on, which way you should move, where you should stand, and so on. There are taped "spots" all over the stage to help you position yourself for the cameras. Some shows will ask you to test the levers or buttons. They want to make sure their digital read-out units, electronic tote boards, and other electrical equipment are fully operational. It's when those lights start flashing and those bells start ringing that your heart really starts jumping!

Follow all instructions given to you by the staff. If they tell you not to step over a yellow line until your name is announced—wait until that moment. An error could result in a very costly or embarrassing delay.

A funny thing happened at one of the tapings of "The Price Is Right" when the contestants were told to shake hands or kiss Bob Barker on the right cheek if they won. It seems that Lawrence, a big 6′3″ L.A. county marshall, didn't want to take any chances when he won. He followed all the instructions to a tee—he shook Bob's hand and kissed him on the right cheek. The crowd roared with laughter, and Bob Barker, who has an exceptionally quick wit, said, "If that's what an L.A. county marshall wants to do, that's all right with me!"

Who Plays and When

After the run-through, all contestants will be asked to wait in the contestant holding room, backstage, or in a special roped-off section of the studio audience. If your show has a holding room, you may be able to watch the contestants currently playing on closed-circuit television. It's a kick to see your new friends play, and you will find yourself cheering them along. Also be sure to make the most of this viewing period by studying the show yet again and becoming even more comfortable with it. When you do, you'll naturally feel more confident and in control when it's your turn to play.

Who decides which contestant plays next? The answer varies from show to show. Although there are a few producers in the industry who let their contestant coordinators make all the selections, on most shows the producer has the final say. Some networks require the producer to put three preselected names into a hat and let their representative randomly pick the person who will play next.

Sometimes producers will pick two people who look similar and flip a coin to decide whom they will use. They may also base their judgment solely on personality. Cheryl Reinwand, winner of $150,000 on "$100,000 Pyramid," felt they picked her to play over the others because she was smiling throughout the entire taping.

Many shows use "contrasting" people. If there's a male already playing, they will choose a female opponent. If there's a young champion, they will use an older challenger. A brunette might be pitted against a blonde. Again, being older, a male, a minority, or an out-of-towner will usually mean that you get chosen sooner. If you're just a "local," you will have to make yourself noticed so that you won't have to come back the next day or week. Regardless of who chooses the contestants and how they do so, you should be at your best and raring to go!

Remember all the guidelines mentioned in chapter 3. Dress nicely and cheerfully. Be friendly, confident, and attentive. Your "presence" must be very evident to the producer or you will not be chosen to play that day.

I really milked the fact that I have a twin sister. On two shows—"Match Game" and "All Star Blitz"—I told the producer and coordinator that she was in the audience. Later in the show the cameras zoomed in on her. On "Child's Play" I told them my fiancé was in the audience. I'm quite sure that it helped me to be chosen to play that day.

Martin Gold from the Bronx knew that the "All Star Blitz" contestant coordinator was looking for a male contestant to play the next game, so he made himself very noticeable by saying laughingly, "Okay, I'm ready to play—pick me!" His confidence paid off. He was selected by the contestant coordinator right then and there and went on to win $6,450!

So take advantage of any "edge" you can think of. Whether you tell the coordinator your parents flew in from Iowa just to see you play or just that you are really so excited to be there, you will give him or her the impression that you are ready and eager to play.

You will never know exactly when you will be asked to "Come on down!" The producer will tell the coordinator who is to be next, and he or she, in turn, will tell you—but only at the very last minute. There are two reasons why they don't want to tell you in advance:

1. They don't want you to become too nervous beforehand;
2. You'll be more excited with that last-minute rush of adrenaline, and it will show.

LIGHTS! CAMERA! ACTION!

The lights grow brighter and the show's theme music begins to play while the audience is being led into the studio. The show's announcer or "warm-up" person greets the audience as they take their seats. It is this person's job to get the audience revved up for the show. He or she starts by making them feel comfortable with questions like, "Is anyone celebrating a birthday or anniversary?" "Anyone visiting us from out of town?" The announcer will tell jokes, play mini mock games, and even give out prizes.

Questions about any or every aspect of the show are asked and answered. Then the announcer introduces the always-charming host and any celebrity players. And after about thirty minutes, the audience is just about going wild with anticipation.

The taping of each show is supposed to match the length of time the show will air on TV—anywhere from twenty-three to twenty-eight minutes—with time left for commercial spots that are inserted later. It is during this relatively short period of time that the producer must squeeze in enough excitement and human interest to make the viewer at home tune in the next day for more.

During the rehearsal and waiting period before the actual taping, there are a number of things you must avoid doing.

Don't:

- Chew gum
- Be loud or obnoxious
- Be hostile to other contestants
- Ask the coordinator too many questions
- Complain about the long wait
- "Act" (just be yourself)
- Talk or whisper to your spouse or others while on stage (including the host, unless, of course, you are actually taping)
- Signal or wave to *anyone* in the audience or on the staff
- Criticize another contestant's playing ability
- Play up to or bother the coordinator
- Touch, hold, clap, or lean into your microphone
- Drum or pound on the game table (this causes static on the tape, and you might have to play a game over again)

Some shows require that you introduce yourself briefly to the host. Others will have the host say a few words about you. This information is taken from your interview(s) and is prepared by the writers or the coordinator. Don't worry that you'll be surprised—you will be told well in advance what to expect.

If you are asked to introduce yourself, use the speech you prepared in your interview. Don't talk about your problems, illnesses, or anything negative. A few shows will let you say "Hi!" to certain people or mention the name of your employer or school, but most of them won't. Your release form should tell you exactly what you can and cannot say.

If the show's host asks you to elaborate on something, just pretend you and he are the only ones present. Don't worry if you are absolutely shaking in your boots—that's normal. Your mind will compensate by reacting faster. Think of it as having an advantage. Bob Hope still gets nervous before he goes in front of a camera. The trick is to make that nervous energy work *for* you, not against you.

When your big moment arrives, you will be fitted with a microphone and escorted onto the stage. You'll experience quite a rush knowing that millions of people will be watching you. You might feel that it's all you can do not to trip over the cables and wires, but armed with the knowledge and confidence you have gained here, you will be ready!

Celebrity-Host Match-Ups

These celebrities hosted game shows throughout the fifties, sixties, and seventies. Match the emcees to the shows they hosted.

Emcee	Game Show
__ **1.** Gary Moore	**A.** "Earn Your Vacation"
__ **2.** Basil Rathbone	**B.** "Snap Judgment"
__ **3.** Vincent Price	**C.** "Jackpot Bowling"
__ **4.** Johnny Carson	**D.** "It Takes Two"
__ **5.** Mike Wallace	**E.** "Concentration"
__ **6.** Milton Berle	**F.** "ESP"
__ **7.** Hugh Downs	**G.** "I've Got a Secret"
__ **8.** Jackie Gleason	**I.** "You're in the Picture"
__ **9.** Vin Scully	**J.** "Your Lucky Clue"
__**10.** Ed McMahon	**K.** "Guess Again"

Answers: 1-G 2-J 3-F 4-A 5-K 6-C 7-E 8-I 9-D 10-B

Chapter 7

Cash, Prizes, and the IRS

When the game ends and you've won a long list of prizes, questions will undoubtedly pop into your head: "What am I going to do with all that patio furniture when I live in an apartment?" "Will I have to pay taxes on that electric spaghetti fork?" "Can I keep the jewelry but give away the five-year supply of lipstick?"

At this point, you must decide what you want to do with the cash, merchandise, or consolation prizes you have won. You will have between three and ten days after your appearance to make that decision, depending on the show. Your five basic options are to keep, exchange, sell, donate, or refuse your winnings.

KEEPING YOUR WINNINGS

If you decide to keep the prizes and/or cash you've won, here is what will happen:

The list of cash and/or merchandise you have won will be sent by the show's prize company on a 1099 form (Miscellaneous Income) directly to the IRS. There is no way of avoiding taxes if you decide to keep the money or prizes.

If you have won cash or prizes on a game show filmed in California, you will be taxed according to the California tax laws, not those of the state where you live. This rule applies to any state where you appear. The cash and prizes you have won will be considered ordinary income, not a capital gain or a gift, so you will have to report them as such, using the 1040 long form.

Cash and/or gift certificates must be declared at the show's stated value. (Gift certificates do not include sales tax.) Merchandise, however, can be declared at its *fair market value,* not at the manufacturer's suggested retail price. Manufacturers often raise the value of their merchandise on game shows for their own tax purposes. Therefore, it would be difficult to get that amount if you sold their products on the open market.

The lower the fair market value, the lower your taxes will be. To determine what the fair market value of a prize is, simply find out the lowest price at which you could purchase the identical item(s). Let's say, for example, that you have just won a beautiful new camper valued at $15,000. If you go to a camper dealership and get written proof that that particular camper is selling for $10,000, you will only be taxed on the current, fair market price of $10,000. (Some shows include tax and license as part of the prize package; others do not.)

Always check discount stores for the lowest possible price of each item—and get it in writing. You can also attach a store ad or a classified ad with the sale price as a "receipt" for the IRS. When I received a case of kitchen cleaner on "Child's Play," I went to my local supermarket to compare costs and obtained a written price quote for considerably less than the manufacturer's suggested retail price. If you make an effort to comparison shop, you will end up paying less in taxes.

If you win jewelry, be sure to get an appraisal from a wholesale jeweler.

If your prize is gold or silver, you will have to declare its value on the day you receive it, even if the gold or silver market drops in the near future.

The audience goes crazy when contestants win a million dollars

When you watch game shows like ''One Million Dollar Chance of a Lifetime,'' you'll see the host hand over thousands of dollars to the winners. But do you know what happens when the taping ends? The contestants must hand back the money. That may sound disappointing, but most of that money is fake anyway. Real bills are put on top of those phony stacks of cash to create an illusion of ''richness.''

What about the furs and rings that are awarded to winners on shows like ''Sale of the Century'' and ''Wheel of Fortune''? Yes, they too are handed back to the prize coordinator. It is rare that a game show will let contestants keep any of the prizes given to them at the studio.

The producer will send you any money you've won in the form of a check within thirty to sixty days after your show *airs*. Merchandise will be shipped by the manufacturer anywhere from thirty to ninety days after your air date, *not* your taping date. This waiting period gives the manufacturer enough time to arrange the necessary delivery details.

If you do not receive your prize(s) within ninety days of the air date, if you receive your prize(s) in a damaged condition, or if they are not the same prizes described on your prize form, call the prize coordinator immediately. He or she will rectify the problem either by calling the manufacturer or having you contact them directly.

Vacations and trips are nontransferable. Only the actual winner and the person of his or her choice can use the airline tickets, hotel vouchers, and so on. This is an old rule dating back to the early TV giveaways when a crowd of people waited backstage to buy the newly won trips. Upon investigation it was later discovered that these people were also falsifying passports and using those tickets to sneak aliens into the country. Unfortunately, this means that if for some reason you cannot go, you will not be able to give the trip to a friend or relative, sell it, or receive cash or credit from the airline.

Most trips must be taken within nine months to a year of the air date and are usually round trip from L.A. or New York. Call your local travel agent to help make connecting arrangements if you live elsewhere. The airline will usually grant three alternate departure dates due to restrictions as to availability, especially during the busy holiday season. Most vacation packages provide a room for two with two meals a day. For items such as telephone calls, gift-store purchases, liquor, room service, and tips, you will be on your own.

Make sure you will be able to use your vacation prize before accepting it. If something will prevent you from going, simply refuse it. It can be pretty depressing to win a Hawaiian vacation that you later discover you can't use, sell, or give away, especially since you will have to pay taxes on it. But if this does happen, try to make it sting a little less by looking at travel brochures or newspapers for less expensive fares. Another good idea is to check with the airlines or travel agencies for any supersaver fares and use that reduced amount as the declared value of the trip for your taxes.

EXCHANGING YOUR WINNINGS

It's like magic! You've become the proud owner of a brand new "fire-engine red" sports car. But when your insurance agent tells you that a red car means bigger premiums because its higher visibility can result in more moving violations, the magic of the moment suddenly disappears. Your agent advises you to try to get another color to keep your insurance costs down. Can you? Yes, sometimes you can.

Game shows work with independent car dealerships rather than with the major manufacturers. Since car dealers tend to be more flexible with details, call and ask them if they will be able to obtain the color you want.

Sometimes you will be given a choice of sizes for prizes like rings, clothing, or bedding. The thirty- to ninety-day waiting period will give you adequate time to think about these choices and to return the choice order form that will be sent to you.

Substitutions will sometimes be made by the manufacturer if the product promoted on the air is out of stock or the specific model is no longer available. If this happens, the supplier must substitute merchandise of equal or greater retail value.

Some shows will offer a cash-equivalent option for the prizes you've won, but it's not common in the industry. When "Let's Make a Deal" "zonked" a contestant with an elephant, the producer never counted on her actually wanting to keep it instead of the new refrigerator they offered her. Apparently, this was the first time a contestant wanted to keep a joke prize, and they weren't prepared. The elephant was on loan, so they couldn't let her have it. To be fair, the producer had to pay her $30,000, which was the going price for elephants at the time.

Nowadays, contestants are given the option of keeping a *small* animal "zonk" or accepting an alternate prize.

If you have any questions about exchanging a prize, speak to the prize coordinator at the studio. It is his or her job to make sure you get everything you deserve.

SELLING YOUR WINNINGS

What if you win a luxurious cabin cruiser but you become seasick whenever you're on water? Or what if you win the ugliest set of recliner chairs ever manufactured? Fear not! You will be permitted to sell any unwanted or unneeded prizes (except trips) for cold, hard cash.

When you sell prizes, you can use your sales price as the declared value and deduct any expenses of the sale on your income tax return. One woman I know won a refrigerator valued at $1,200. She advertised it at $800 because that was the going price for similar refrigerators being advertised. It took her four months to sell that refrigerator, but she was able to declare it at the fair market value of $800 and deduct all her advertising costs.

There may also be instances where you will be able to write off expenses directly related to receiving or utilizing your prizes. One contestant I interviewed had to rent a trailer in order to pick up the boat she had won. Since this was a necessary expense, she was able to deduct the entire rental fee.

The first thing you should do before selling a prize is to check the classified section of your local newspaper for similar items. By learning the going rate, you can determine what your selling price should be. You can advertise your prize(s) in newspapers, on bulletin boards at colleges or supermarkets, or just by word of mouth. Check your release form to see if you can mention the show's name in the ad. Most shows will allow you only to say "won on a game show." No matter which way you decide to sell your prize, you'll still come out financially ahead.

DONATING YOUR WINNINGS

Donating a prize is like refusing it in a sense, but you have the satisfaction of knowing that it's going to a worthwhile cause. As mentioned earlier, I won a Salvador Dali lithograph suite valued at $4,000 on "All Star Blitz." My husband wanted me to reject it since we would have to pay approximately $2,000 in taxes if we kept the prize. I fought him because the prize had sentimental value for me (even though I've never really been a Dali admirer).

Seven months later my husband and I both grew tired of the Dali art, so he convinced me to give the lithographs to someone who would enjoy them without any tax consequences to us. He suggested that we donate them to my favorite nonprofit group, Volunteer Services to Animals. We declared the fair market value (in this case we used the show's suggested retail price of $4,000) under "other income" and then deducted that amount under "charitable contributions." The two ended up canceling each other out, resulting in no tax ramifications whatsoever. The best part of the transaction was the wonderful grand prize those lithos made for my group's raffle.

If you decide to declare your prizes as "income" and then as a "contribution" in the same amount, the IRS usually won't argue with you. However, the law does state that if you receive a prize valued at more than $5,000, you must provide the IRS with a written appraisal of it.

The new tax laws will not permit "charitable contribution" deductions for those who do not itemize. And since many taxpayers do not have to itemize their deductions, it could cost money to contribute a prize, rather than refuse it. The best thing to do if you have any questions regarding the taxes on your winnings is to check with your accountant.

REFUSING YOUR WINNINGS

The only reasons to refuse a prize are: (1) you cannot afford to pay the taxes on it or (2) it would just be too difficult to sell.

It's a crime when someone wins a new Cadillac convertible and has to give it back, but unfortunately it happens. Trying to sell the car for cash could be a long and frustrating process.

I once won a year's supply of ice cream bars as part of a game show's parting gifts. I felt it best to refuse the prize so I would not be taxed on the $125 value (to say nothing of all those calories)!

There's no reason in the world to refuse cash. No matter what tax bracket you're in, you'll always end up ahead with a cash prize.

WRITE-OFFS

You can write off some game show expenses, such as parking, mileage, lodging, and related phone calls, but you must provide the bills or receipts as proof. Under the new tax law, meals are only 80 percent deductible. Although you can write off all advertising expenditures necessary to sell your prize(s), you must prove that all those expenses were directly related to the sale of those prizes.

While the tax laws concerning the deduction of airfare for interviewing or taping game shows are complex, they basically state that you can only deduct to the extent of your winnings. For example, if your airfare cost $700, and you only won $200 (in cash or the fair market value of your prizes), your deduction would be limited to $200. You should also keep in mind that if you won $20,000 in one day on an out-of-state game show and you were bold enough to deduct expenses for a two-week vacation, you will be sending up a "red flag" to the IRS—so be careful.

Chapter 8

Life After Your First Game Show

Whether you've won or lost on your first game show, the industry will consider you a professional. After waiting the mandatory twelve months, you should have absolutely no problem getting on other game shows because the contestant coordinators will see you as a seasoned competitor, who will not be as nervous as someone on their first show. Coordinators love to find second-timers, since producers are always searching for tried-and-true game players.

FILMING PILOT GAME SHOWS

After your show has aired, you may receive invitations from production companies to film pilots for future game shows. Producers and packagers need to make pilots to pitch their shows to the networks effectively. Judging from the quality of this presentation, a network will decide if it should honor the show with a contract. That is why producers only want to use experienced players for pilots.

I have been asked to film eight pilots, and each production company offered me different terms. Some will want to interview first and then select people to play their game. Others will have you go directly to the studio to play a rehearsal game, and the producer will then determine if he or she wants you for the actual taping.

If you are asked to film a pilot, ask them what they will pay you and how long it will take—don't be shy! I have been offered anywhere from $100 to $250 a day. That sounds pretty good, doesn't it? Well, in one case they wanted me to come down for two interviews, each lasting "hopefully only one hour," and a studio taping lasting up to five hours. I wasn't able to do it because of my busy work schedule.

I did decide to try out for one pilot but only after the coordinator really enticed me. He said I would be paid $100 for going down to the studio and $250 if I was chosen to play the game on tape. The entire taping was only supposed to last three hours, but lo and behold, those three hours turned into six because of the many technical delays.

Some producers are frugal, while others are more generous. Some are even flexible with their terms. When one producer asked me to do a pilot for $50, I told him that it would cost me more than that to take the day off from work. He then offered me $100 and lunch. Another time I was offered $20 and a McDonald's lunch just to come down and play a new game for forty-five minutes in front of the production staff. They wanted an experienced player's opinion of the game: Was it too hard? Was it enjoyable? I had a good time being a guinea pig although I thought the game was juvenile (and I told them so!).

Tammie Eisele, a $22,400 winner on "All Star Blitz," was paid $125 to film a pilot for a game show called "Bargain Hunters." She met lots of people, had a good time, and the entire filming lasted only a few hours.

Mark Fogarty won $6,750 on "Scrabble." They called him a few weeks after the show's taping and asked if he would help work out some changes in the "Scrabble" format. He did and was paid $20 for a half hour of what Mark termed "pure fun!"

The going rate in Hollywood for filming a pilot is $75 a day. If you have the time and could use the money, taping a pilot could be an easy way for you to make some extra cash. You may also be approached by a producer to film a pilot for no money but with the promise of becoming a contestant once the game is sold. It's up to you to decide whether you want to chance it. The worst thing that could happen is that you will have fun playing the game and meeting new people.

SUDDENLY YOU'RE FAMOUS!

If you win *big*, you may be bombarded with requests for interviews and asked to appear on talk shows. It happened to the Rutenbars after they were the first couple to win the million dollars on "One Million Dollar Chance of a Lifetime." The production company sent limos to pick up their entire family before filming their third and last show. They were later flown to Chicago as featured guests on "The Oprah Winfrey Show." They stayed in a beautiful hotel where all their meals and expenses were paid for. Various newspapers interviewed them, and they were even offered a commercial contract.

Many of the contestants I've spoken to have been interviewed by TV reporters, newspapers, and game and news magazines. If you're a good writer, you can even get paid to write about your winning game show experiences for publications like *Reader's Digest* and *Woman's Day*. Many game production-company positions have been filled by former players, too.

There is really no end to the wonderful benefits you can derive from being on a game show!

Contestant Testimonial

LIVING IN THE LIMELIGHT

SUE HENSLEY, Cypress, California

Winner of $24,000 in cash and prizes on ''Joker's Wild,'' ''Liar's Club,'' ''Hollywood Squares,'' and ''All Star Blitz''

''I love game shows—always have! I'll never forget the day I was feeding my baby and watching a game show on TV when something inside my brain just clicked. I said to myself, 'If all these other people can get on a game show and win, why not me?'

''So I tried out for 'The Joker's Wild,' made it through a real tough interview and test, got on, and stayed on for the entire week. I won $3,300 cash, a trip to Hong Kong, and many other great prizes.

''It was an unbelievable time for me. People from all over recognized me from my appearance on the show. One month after my show aired, we took the family to Disneyland, and a girl selling Mickey Mouse hats said she remembered me and had rooted for me all week long.

''A few months later I was dragging my screaming little boy out of a department store when a nice elderly man held the door open for me. He turned to his wife and said, 'This lady played on ''Joker's Wild.'' Remember how we cheered for her?'

''But the most incredible time was when my husband and I were on our trip to Hong Kong. We were in a very small Hong Kong restaurant, waiting to be seated, when a sailor and his wife sat next to us. For some reason the sailor would not stop staring at me. Finally, we all started talking about how we had come to be in Hong Kong. My husband explained that I had won the trip on a TV game show. The sailor asked me what

(continued on next page)

show it was and when it was on. When I told him, he breathed a sigh of relief and said, 'I knew I recognized you from somewhere. I felt uncomfortable saying I knew you in front of my wife when I couldn't remember where we had met. I was on leave the week you were on, and I rooted for you the whole time!'

"For a while it seemed that no matter where I went, I couldn't be anonymous—I felt like a movie star!"

Chapter 9

How a TV Game Show Is Produced

The fierce competition between producers searching for the "perfect" game show is never ending. The networks have piles of game shows that took months, sometimes even years, to produce but for some reason didn't make it. Perhaps the timing wasn't right, or the executives couldn't agree, or maybe something better came along at the same time. Who knows? For every game show that gets on the air, at least fifty do not. Even if a producer has a great game show idea, if he or she doesn't have the technical, financial, and production experience necessary to make it work, a network probably won't take the risk. Networks look for shows that combine good, wholesome entertainment with just the right amount of drama, an element of suspense, a touch of humor, and above all, "real people." All the ringing bells, flashing lights, and fabulous prizes in the world can't disguise a dull or weak game.

Producers or packagers start by verbally presenting their game show idea to a network. If the network likes the idea, a deal will be made to develop it. In most cases the network will give the producer a limited amount of time (usually two months) and a limited budget (usually $10,000 to $20,000) to develop the show. The money is used for a run-through, which can eventually lead to a pilot (which costs anywhere from $250,000 to $500,000 to produce), and then hopefully to a spot on the TV schedule.

If a show makes it to syndication (meaning it's aired nationally), it can make $40,000 a week net and sometimes between $5 million and $20 million a year net. The payoff for a network show is smaller but still substantial. Contracts are usually granted for thirteen weeks, and the renewal length varies, depending on the ever-important ratings.

If you watch a show that has been on the air for a long period of time, you might see occasional format changes. This happens when the producer or network feels that a new look will liven up the show, which in turn will beef up the ratings.

THE PEOPLE BEHIND THE SCENES

It takes a tremendous amount of time and personnel to put together a seemingly uncomplicated game show. Anywhere from 50 to 60 people work more than 200 hours to deliver that half-hour show.

A game show producer is responsible for virtually everything that concerns the running of the show, including the way the game is played and its rules, what prizes are offered, the hiring and firing of the celebrities and production staff, selecting the contestants, the set design, staying within budget, and most important, the show's continuing popularity.

A typical day in the life of a producer is filled with hectic last-minute changes, disrupting phone calls, and frantic staff meetings—hardly the glamorous job most people make it out to be. Most of the producers I know tell me that their jobs are so all-encompassing, they end up living, sleeping, and breathing their shows.

The associate producer acts as a sort of vice-president, taking care of check lists, cue cards, and perhaps even writing ques-

Guest game show host Jim Peck graciously holds up the cue card for the "Crosswits" announcer

tions and puzzles. And he or she must always be ready to take charge in case the producer can't.

As I explained earlier, contestant coordinators act as caretaker, watchdog, guardian and protector for their contestants. It's hard to imagine that they end up reassuring, congratulating, and consoling literally thousands of people yearly, but they do!

People from all over the country write in about everything from the length of a contestant's skirt to their belief that they would make the perfect host or hostess for the show. Viewer correspondence alone can keep one office worker busy.

Prize brokers handle the negotiations between the manufacturers and the production companies for all merchandise. Shows must pay for the cars and trips they give away, receiving nothing but a discount on the price tag. They usually accumulate the money to do this by deducting a percentage of the fee income for the prize brokerage firm and placing it into a special "prize account." Some networks, such as CBS, have an in-house department that does all the prize buying.

Major appliances like televisions, stereos, and furniture are usually exchanged for free promotion or can be purchased for less than the wholesale price, depending upon the cost of the product. Smaller appliances are also given away for free promotion. Suppliers of lower-priced merchandise such as food, cosmetics, and paint normally pay a standard fee for the privilege of promoting their wares on TV. The fees paid for these smaller items often end up paying for some of the bigger, more expensive prizes.

Several directors are assigned to every game show. They are in charge of the audio, visual, technical, and lighting aspects and, of course, the overall filming of the game. For the most part, viewers and contestants aren't aware of the many taping problems that occur, because the crew corrects them before they get out of hand.

Of course, there are times when technical problems do become troublesome. Hugh Downs wasn't thrilled when he was hosting "Concentration," and a fire broke out from behind one of the turning squares. And host Jim Peck got a little perturbed when he tripped over an unstable staircase while walking onto the "Big Showdown" set. But all in all, technicians do a fine job of troubleshooting, and their many talents and abilities contribute to the game's overall success.

If taping takes place in the morning, a stagehand's "day"

begins around midnight. The stagehands work with the scenic designers to put together the set. Then the lighting director and his crew come in to hang and focus all the high-watt lamps. At about 5:00 A.M. the audio director and his team appear to hook up the speakers and microphones for the host, contestants, audience, and special sound effects. The video director and camera people arrive a bit later to set up and adjust the camera control panels. There are usually ten to twenty people working in the control room. They log in the commercials, operate and maintain the technical equipment, decide what camera angles to use, check scripts, and censor anything they believe is inappropriate.

Merchandising coordinators then work hand in hand with scenic designers to display the prizes in the most appealing way possible. (A diamond necklace certainly looks better on the neck of a beautiful model than in a box!) It's amazing what these stage technicians can do with a little cardboard, plywood, and plastic. They work hard to create a vision of tinsel and glitter for the home audience.

There are also carpenters, painters, caterers, makeup artists, wardrobe people, and many, many more, all of whom make up the production team. Sometimes when visiting a set, you will see stage people doing what appears to be nothing, but everyone has a function, and they work hard at it.

Writers are hired to pore through encyclopedias and other sources searching for just the right information and puzzles. These talented people turn facts into interesting and often amusing questions. A game show will fail if too many of the questions go unanswered, so it is the writer's responsibility to see that the questions are never too difficult to answer or the puzzles too obscure to solve.

After appearing as a contestant on "All Star Blitz," I tried out to become a writer for the show. I was hired and quickly discovered just how grueling it can be to write questions week after week. Out of the 200 questions and answers I submitted each week, Merrill Heatter, the executive producer, and David

On the set of "$100,000 Pyramid"

Greenfield, the producer, used 5 to 10 of the best. They did the same with the other three writers to accumulate the 40 questions needed weekly. It was quite a challenge.

You would also be amazed at the amount of paperwork involved in producing a game show. Detailed records must be maintained on every contestant, including the money won, prizes awarded, questions answered, as well as all relevant contracts. And, manufacturers must be notified as to the size, color, and delivery date of all prizes.

RECIPE FOR A SUCCESSFUL GAME SHOW

Former game show producer Norman Blumenthal wrote the following amusing recipe for producing a successful game show:

4 contestants (vary with type of show)
165 pounds of ham (emcee brand)
150 pounds of announcer (deep-voice type)
250 good-natured people in audience (all shapes)
1 ton of prizes (best available)
some cheesecake (2 gorgeous female models)
1 cup of humor (very dry)
1 cup of pathos (very wet)
dash of greed
½ teaspoon game

Prepare all ingredients in advance, selecting only the finest quality available. Slowly cook raw contestants in uncomfortable seats until tender. Drain off excess sweat from hands and forehead. Stir in grated ham. Add bits of dried humor while combining with crushed pathos. Wherever possible, scatter in a little game (use sparingly, being careful not to overenrich mixture).

Season to taste by sprinkling in studio gasps, applause, and a dash of laughter (canned or live). Scoop in mounds of merchandise prizes, slowly but steadily. Baste frequently with flashing lights and loud musical fanfares, bells, gongs, buzzers, and whistles. Blend in greed. Mix well.

Beat one contestant well and let simmer. Pour ton of prizes over the other. Use cheesecake to add zest and eye appeal. Repeat process with new contestant. Bake at 90 degrees under hot lights for about ½ hour. Serves 40 to 60 million.

Name That Game

Match these ten familiar game-show phrases with their show.

	Phrase	Game Show
__	**A.** "Sign in, please"	**1.** "Hollywood Squares"
__	**B.** "The secret word is . . ."	**2.** "Joker's Wild"
__	**C.** "Is it bigger than a breadbox?"	**3.** "Gambit"
__	**D.** "Number one, what is your name, please?"	**4.** "What's My Line?"
__	**E.** "Come on down!"	**5.** "The Price Is Right"
__	**F.** "Numbers 5 and 2"	**6.** "I've Got a Secret"
__	**G.** "Hello, stars."	**7.** "You Bet Your Life"
__	**H.** "Watch out for the bankrupt"	**8.** "Concentration"
__	**I.** "50, 50, Joker"	**9.** "Wheel of Fortune"
__	**J.** "Any 21 wins our jackpot"	**10.** "To Tell the Truth"

Answers: A-4, B-7, C-6, D-10, E-5, F-8, G-1, H-9, I-2, J-3

Chapter 10

The History of TV Game Shows

Contests, games, giveaways and lotteries have been around practically since the dawn of man—certainly long before television. There has always been a special allure to winning this kind of competition. It's easy—almost like getting something for nothing (though we all know that's impossible). You don't have to be especially smart or talented—you just have to be you!

The first game shows became part of our lives during the early days of radio. They entertained, educated, astounded, and often touched us profoundly. Over the past five decades we have watched their evolution into the entertainment phenomenon they are today. Their names are familiar, and along with the faces of the personalities who have made them great, they ring bells and buzzers in our hearts and minds.

What were game shows like before TV? For the $64 answer, we must travel back to the golden age of radio in 1936 to look in on "Professor Quiz," one of America's first quiz shows.

Each week, Professor Quiz (real identity: Craig Earl) selected a contestant to appear on stage with him and answer various questions. If the contestant answered correctly, he or she received a prize—a whopping five dollars. Soon all of America was tuning in to laugh and play along.

Throughout the early thirties, "The Major Bowes Family Hour" and his "Original Amateur Hour" brought members of the studio audience up on stage to participate in humorous interviews before taking part in a talent contest. Winners on the Major Bowes shows were determined by the spin of the "wheel of fortune"; losers were dismissed with a "gong."

Sound familiar? It should! Some forty years later Merv Griffin and Chuck Barris made millions with "Wheel of Fortune" and "The Gong Show." Some of the fine talents on those early shows became huge successes too; a perky little singer named Belle (Bubbles) Silverman for one, who later changed her name to Beverly Sills and took the New York City Opera by storm.

By the late thirties there were more than thirty quiz shows on the air. Contestants could "Break the Bank," "Stop the Music," "Beat the Band," or go for a "Chance of a Lifetime" and win as much as fifty brand-new one-dollar bills plus two cartons of Raleigh cigarettes (the sponsor's product, of course).

Some of the more successful shows were "Dr. I.Q.," where contestants could win up to seventy-five silver dollars; "Melody Puzzles," the first radio quiz to add music to its format; "Battle of the Sexes," an early, humorous panel game; and "What's My Name?" the show that marked the quiz-show debut of Arlene Francis.

It was at this time that producers realized that if the sound of silver dollars, cash registers, and music boosted listenership, the sound of the telephone might be even more enticing. It proved to be just that.

"Pot O' Gold" was the first quiz show to call listeners at home and award a cumulative jackpot—an element that is used in many game shows today. Each week the show placed a call to "a lucky person somewhere in America," and then the orchestra, led by Horance Heidt, played a popular tune. If the contestant could name the song title correctly, he or she would win all the money that had accumulated in the jackpot since the last correct answer.

In 1941 quiz shows were a proven hit—more than eighty shows debuted that year or shortly thereafter. Three refreshingly young radio personalities came on the scene and totally changed the look and style of quiz shows—Ralph Edwards, Art Linkletter, and Mark Goodson.

"Professor Quiz" awards a contestant a grand prize of $5 for correctly answering a question

Edwards was the creator and host of "This Is Your Life" and "Truth or Consequences," radio and television staples that lasted some thirty years.

Linkletter and his partner John Guedel created "People Are Funny," which started on radio in 1941 and ended seventeen years later on television. Around the same time Linkletter and Guedel also created "House Party," which was a hit for more than twenty-five years on both radio and television.

Goodson's success in game shows came five years later in 1946. But it was during this time period that he wrote and directed several successful soap operas while "pitching" his game show concepts whenever possible. (He was turned down time after time.)

By 1946 the war was over, television was emerging as a powerful force, and game shows were riding on its coattails. That year Mark Goodson and Bill Todman joined forces and sold their first game show, "Winner Take All." Bill Cullen became the emcee, and his close relationship with Mark Goodson still flourishes today—more than forty years later!

Jack Barry and Dan Enright were also selling their panel and game shows in 1946. Fortune smiled on them the next year when they sold the very popular "Juvenile Jury."

The game show craze was primarily a daytime phenomenon in the forties and didn't really take off on TV until the big money shows came to prime time in the early fifties. During this period, Goodson and Todman were crowned the game show leaders. Their hits included the three-time Emmy-award-winning "What's My Line?" which aired for more than twenty-four years (TV's longest running prime-time game show). Its mystery guests included hundreds of "personalities"—including Frank Sinatra, Gary Cooper, Bette Davis, Charlton Heston, Paul Newman, Elizabeth Taylor, Woody Allen, Clint Eastwood, Lassie, and Marlon Brando—all of whom were happy to "sign in, please."

Other Goodson and Todman favorites included "I've Got a Secret," a show where celebrity panelists tried to guess the contestants' secrets; "Beat the Clock," where couples were required to perform various stunts, usually within thirty seconds; "To Tell the Truth," where a panel of four celebrities tried to determine which of the three guests, each claiming to be the same person, was telling the truth; and "The Price Is Right," a merchandise-pricing game originally hosted by Bill Cullen that is still riding high in the top five today!

Other production companies had hits with "Name That Tune," "Strike It Rich," "Break the Bank," "Queen for a Day," "You Bet Your Life," "Dough Re Mi," "Tic Tac Dough," "The Big Pay Off," "It Could Be You," and many, many more.

In the late 1950s new games came on the scene that asked more difficult questions than their counterparts of the past three decades. The incentives for winning were much greater too, of course. Games like "The $64,000 Question," "The $64,000 Challenge," "The $100,000 Big Surprise," "Dotto," "High-Low," and "Twenty-One" (an electric version of the card game Black Jack), with virtually no limit on the amount of money that could be won, turned out to be goldmines for their production companies as well as their contestants. Television critics of the fifties said these games were the best around—but also the "crookedest."

During this period, game shows became a national obsession, drawing ratings unequaled until J.R. was shot on "Dallas" some twenty-five years later. Then, enter if you please, "the quiz show scandals." When all was finally revealed, the nation's confidence had been betrayed to a degree that can only be compared to Watergate.

Mr. Edward Hilgemeier, a contestant-to-be on the show "Dotto," a video adaptation of connect-the-dots that aired in 1958, was the first to blow the whistle. Mr. Hilgemeier was waiting for his turn to play when he noticed one of the other contestants looking through some notes. When she went on stage, she innocently left the notes behind. Glancing at them quickly, Mr. Hilgemeier found that they were the answers to the questions the woman was asked on the show. He was flabbergasted. He showed the answers to the losing contestant,

The old "Movie Game" gang—*counter-clockwise from bottom left:* Carl Reiner, Liz Scott, John Wayne, Ann Sothern, Sonny Fox, and Army Archard

and they marched angrily into the producer's office. Caught red-handed, the producer allegedly offered to bribe the losing contestant with $14,000 and Mr. Hilgemeier with a mere $1,500 to remain silent. Totally astounded, Mr. Hilgemeier and the losing contestant left the producer's office emptyhanded. Mr. Hilgemeier immediately notified the network of the scam. They thanked him for coming forward and promised to look into it.

The next bomb dropped when "Twenty-One" contestant Herb Stempel revealed that the producer had asked him to play the part of a down-and-out G.I. by wearing a shabby suit and acting "pitiful" once in the isolation booth. He was given the answers to the questions beforehand, and after winning $49,000 was told to "take a dive" because he was no longer useful. Stempel was also paid $18,500 up front, before he first appeared on the show and won the $49,000. Amazing isn't it?

But the scandal did not stop there. As time went on, more and more disgruntled ex-contestants from different game shows came forward with tales of suspicion and trickery. Investigations started immediately. The general public was intrigued; this type of deception was something everyone could relate to, and they didn't like it one bit!

In August of 1957, *Look* magazine broke the first stories of behind-the-scenes string-pulling on the game and quiz shows all America loved. They revealed that an astonishing number of these shows were rigged, including "The $64,000 Question," "The $64,000 Challenge," "Twenty-One," "Tic Tac Dough," "Treasure Hunt," "Dotto," "High-Low," and "You Bet Your Life" with Groucho Marx. Band leader Xavier Cugat confessed that he was coached on "The $64,000 Challenge." Patty Duke's manager admitted that he paid $1,000 to the celebrity talent coordinator of "The $64,000 Challenge" to get Duke on the show.

When Charles Van Doren, a young genius and prize-winning poet, appeared on the show "Twenty-One," it broke all network ratings. But the bubble broke when he later apologetically announced that he had been given the answers by the show's creator and producer, Dan Enright. Mr. Van Doren was told by Enright, "We need you to replace the champion. He's too dull. Don't worry about it though, contestants are fed the answers every day."

As the testimonies continued to pour in, and the ratings began to slip, networks started panicking. Both CBS and NBC canceled all their big-money quizzes. Gone were "Dotto," "Top Dollar," "The Big Payoff," "Name That Tune," "The $64,000 Question," "The $64,000 Challenge," "Twenty-One," and "High-Low."

The sponsors were paying high prices to have their products promoted, and they were not willing to settle for low ratings.

Frightened producers began sealing contestants in soundproof boxes. Anyone connected with the presentation of game shows was forced to sign lengthy affidavits attesting to their honesty—or they were immediately dismissed.

By the time the hearings came to an end, the public was quite disenchanted with game shows, and all the big-money shows that had been so popular were gone from both daytime and prime-time television. After the hearings, President Eisenhower addressed the country and compared the quiz-show scandals to the "black sox" scandal in baseball back in 1917. "What a terrible thing to do to the American public," he declared.

It took a long time to restore the public's faith in game shows, but by the mid-sixties, they were back in favor. New production companies like Hatos/Hall, Ralph Andrews, Chuck Barris, Heatter/Quigley, Merv Griffin, and Bob Stewart, were starting to give Goodson and Todman, John Guedel, and Barry and Enright a run for their money.

Monty Hall, along with partner Stephan Hatos, created "Let's Make a Deal," a show that had a record-breaking run in both daytime and prime-time slots during the sixties and early seventies. This talented team went on to create other popular shows too, including "Split Second" and "It's Anybody's Guess."

Ralph Andrews had more than four shows on TV at once. His creative crew developed such network hits as "You Don't Say," starring Tom Kennedy, "I'll Bet," with Jack Narz, "Liar's Club," with Rod Serling, and "It Takes Two," with Vin Scully.

The sixties proved to be a period of growth and creativity for game shows. The difficult and often dull question-and-answer games were a thing of the past. Refreshing new formats and entertaining concepts were dangled in front of the viewers' eyes, and they ate them up! Turning on the TV was like entering a supermarket: you could feast on a virtual cornucopia of nonfattening (but certainly habit-forming) game shows! The home audience could watch married couples predicting how well they knew their spouses, people agreeing and disagreeing with Hollywood celebrities, and curtains being lifted to reveal prizes such as camels and pigs.

In 1965 Chuck Barris, a creative young man with an original mind and a sensitivity to people, hit the scene with "The Dating Game," hosted by Jim Lange, and "The Newlywed Game," hosted by Bob Eubanks. Both shows ended up making the long, hard jump to prime-time. By 1968 Barris Productions had more than six shows on the air. Chuck Barris made the pages of *Life* magazine and managed to seduce some of the TV and movie's biggest stars to appear on "The Dating Game": Tom Selleck, Burt Reynolds, Farrah Fawcett, Mama Cass, Groucho Marx, Phyllis Diller, The Bee Gees, and even Michael Jackson, to name just a few.

By the mid-sixties Merv Griffin had developed a solid hit with "Jeopardy!," hosted by Art Fleming. Merrill Heater and Bob Quigley were rolling with shows like "Hollywood Squares," "Gambit," and "High Rollers." And Bob Stewart was doing well with "Eye Guess," "3 on a Match," "You're Putting Me On," "Personality," and "The $10,000 Pyramid."

Looking back, the biggest hits of the sixties turned out to be "Truth or Consequences," "The Price Is Right," "Concentration," "Let's Make a Deal," "Password," "Jeopardy!," "Hollywood Squares," "Match Game," "The Dating Game," "The Newlywed Game," "Sale of the Century," "Say When," "Eye Guess," and "You Don't Say."

The host fraternity at the time included Bob Barker, Monty Hall, Art James, Art Fleming, Allen Ludden, Tom Kennedy, Jim Lange, Bob Eubanks, Bob Clayton, Gene Rayburn, and Peter Marshall. Their relaxed manners, smooth voices, and good looks still look good in the eighties—some twenty years later. As a result of the stigma cast by the game show scandals, emcees Hal March, Ralph Story, Jack Barry, and Jack Narz had to put their careers on hold . . . but not forever. By the late seventies Jack Narz was successfully hosting several shows at once, and Jack Barry was busy producing "The New Tic Tac Dough" as well as hosting and producing "The Joker's Wild."

Game show hosts square off on a "Family Feud" special for charity

In the seventies new emcees like Alex Trebek, Jim Perry, Jim Peck, Richard Dawson, Chuck Woolery, Geoff Edwards, Dick Clark, Bert Convy, and Chuck Barris won the hearts of American housewives, while old favorites such as Bill Cullen, Dennis James, Wink Martindale, and others were still very much around. It appeared that there was a game show for everyone.

Statistics show that every year more than 50,000 ordinary people just like you and me try out to become contestants, and more than 85 million people watch game shows daily. Not only do these millions of people watch and play along with the contestants on TV, they also run out and purchase the home version of their favorites, so they can play with their families and friends. A home game usually doesn't become financially feasible until after the game show has been on TV for a minimum of three years, however, thereby proving its stability.

If you were to ask Wink, Alex, Bill, Pat, Vanna, Monty, or Bob why game shows are so popular, they would tell you that it's hard to put your finger on it, but most successful games are easy to understand, fun to play along with, and, of course, it's always nice to see something good happen to people.

The games of the eighties aren't any harder to play than those in times past, but they are faster! And with the increased speed come increased prizes—at last count up to one million dollars! Old games like "High Rollers," "Jeopardy!," and "Concentration" have been recycled and are big hits once again. Good-looking new hosts like Bill Rafferty, Peter Tomarken, and Pat Sajak have become the hearththrobs of countless women. And the overwhelmingly popular hostess Vanna White from "Wheel of Fortune" has become a household name.

Looking a little closer at the game show's general ingredients, we see that approximately every seven seconds something happens—a question is asked or answered, bells ring, buttons buzz, lights flash, and prizes are displayed. Then, on top of all that excitement, attractive hosts and hostesses serve as icing on the cake.

Throughout the sixties, seventies, and eighties, there has always been an average of at least fifteen syndicated and network games successfully competing against the sitcoms and dramas on TV. Viewers may easily lose themselves in power and lust on serials like "Dynasty" and "Dallas," but no show fulfills someone's fantasies quite like a game show!

Popular hostess Vanna White backstage on "Wheel of Fortune"

Merv and the Wheel

Once upon a time a man named Merv Griffin invented a game show called "Wheel of Fortune." Chuck Woolery became the host, and the show did fairly well in the ratings. After a period of time Chuck had to leave, so Merv had to find a new emcee for his game show. It was one fine day soon thereafter that Merv spotted a funny local L.A. news weatherman by the name of Pat Sajak. Merv said, "Pat, I need a host for my game show. I'll pay you a lot of money if you will only say yes!" Pat smiled and said, "Indeed I will!"

Merv then decided he needed a new hostess for his game. He interviewed hundreds of girls until he saw one that was "just right." Her name was Vanna White, and she was an ex-cheerleader from South Carolina's North Myrtle Beach.

TV viewers began sending Pat and Vanna thousands of fan letters each week, and they were soon crowned the king and queen of game showdom. Pat made a jolly good king and Vanna took her job as queen very seriously, for she knew that she was a role model for young girls everywhere. She started writing books, posing for posters, taping videos, filming commercials, and even developing a cartoon series that lead to Vanna dolls, toy houses, and vans.

Millions of fans (or "Wheelies" as they liked to call themselves) tuned in to watch "Wheel," which made it the highest rated syndicated series in TV history. Every year Merv would spend $8 million to produce his show, but he didn't mind since he made a tidy $115 million in gross revenues. As a matter of fact, Merv was so pleased with the success of "Wheel of Fortune" that he decreed, "As long as the 'Wheel' keeps spinning, everyone will live happily ever after!"

Appendix

Practice Word Clues, Puzzles, and Questions

Use these practice tests to sharpen your knowledge retention, puzzle solving, and word communication skills. They are rated easy, moderately difficult, and hard.

EASY WORD CLUES

These clues are similar to those used on the "$25,000 Pyramid." The clues on the left describe a single word. Fill in that word on the right.

Describe these things you can be thankful for:

1. This is my . . . (pointing to other player) __________
2. Not the parent but the . . . ____________________
3. You win the Academy . . . ____________________
4. If you are Jewish or Catholic, that is your . . . ______
5. You win this to go to college; it is a . . . __________

6. You pull the handle and win a . . . ______________

7. You work out and take vitamins so you're in good . . . ______________

8. It comes in dollar bills and coins; it is . . . ______________

9. Your marriage partner is your . . . ______________

10. Pretty or handsome is . . . ______________

Answers: **1.** friend **2.** child **3.** award **4.** religion **5.** scholarship **6.** jack-pot **7.** health **8.** money **9.** spouse **10.** good-looking

MODERATELY DIFFICULT WORD CLUES

These word clues are similar to those used on "Password." Each two-word clue on the left describes another word. Fill in that word on the right.

1. hate (voice inflection—opposite), *amore* ______________

2. automobile, German ______________

3. May, month (voice inflection—leads to) ______________

4. bird, endangered ______________

5. Theodore, President ______________

6. hominy, Southern ______________

7. instrument, mouth ______________

8. out (voice inflection—opposite) ______________

9. Amazon, tropical ______________

10. pot, tea ______________

11. roar, mane ______________

12. puppets, TV ______________

Answers: **1.** love **2.** Volkswagen **3.** June **4.** eagle **5.** Roosevelt **6.** grits **7.** harmonica **8.** in **9.** jungle **10.** kettle **11.** lion **12.** Muppets

HARD WORD CLUES

Clues 1 through 5 are similar to those used in the "Pyramid" bonus game. Begin your answer with a phrase like, "Things having to do with . . ."

1. Your wallet, your keys, your change __________

2. Insults, criticism __________

3. A bride's linen, a bride's dress __________

4. Granola, trees, nonpreservatives __________

5. Your car's ignition, a wind-up toy __________

Circle the correct definition for words 6 through 9 for these questions, which are similar to those used on "Word Play."

6. A "derogation" is **(a)** a plumbing leak **(b)** a loss of rank **(c)** an insult

7. "farina" is **(a)** ground corn **(b)** Italian bread **(c)** Brazilian nut

8. "raze" means **(a)** to kill **(b)** to shave **(c)** to cooperate

9. "valgus" is **(a)** a hike up a hill **(b)** a twisted position **(c)** an insect

Clues 10 through 12 are similar to those used on "Double Talk." Combine the two clues to determine the word they are describing.

10. Any insect, hidden microphone = __________

11. To energize, a bully = __________

12. A fruit, a sound of disapproval = __________

Answers: **1.** Things that you put in your pocket **2.** Things that would hurt someone's feelings **3.** Things that are white **4.** Things that are natural **5.** Things that are started **6.** b **7.** a **8.** b **9.** b **10.** bug **11.** daunt **12.** raspberry

EASY PUZZLES

These puzzles are from "One Million Dollar Chance of a Lifetime."

1. 8 words—place

_ r _ _ w _ y,
_ e _ u e _ t,
_ i r _ c _ i _ n _,
_ o _ f _ s _ o _ =
D _   y _ _   _ _ _ w
_ h _   _ _ y   _ o
S _ _   J _ _ _?

2. 2 words—person

_ o w _ _ f _ l,
b _ b l _ _ a _,
_ h _ r _ _ t e r,
f _ l m _ _ t _ r =
C _ a _ l _ _ n
H _ _ t _ n

3. 4 words—person

r _ s c _ _,
_ r _ g _ n,
_ n _ g h _,
_ r m _ _ = a
d _ _ s _ l   _ n
d _ s _ _ _ s s

Puzzles 4 through 8 are similar to those used on "Wheel of Fortune" and pertain to "bubbling things."

4. _ h _ _ p _ g _ e
5. _ e _ _ z e r

6. h _ t   _ p r _ _ g s
7. _ o l _ e n   _ a _ a
8. s _ d _   _ o p

Answers: 1. freeway, request, directions, confusion = Do you know the way to San Jose? **2.** powerful, biblical, character, film star = Charlton Heston **3.** rescue, dragon, knight, armor = a damsel in distress **4.** champagne **5.** seltzer **6.** hot springs **7.** molten lava **8.** soda pop

MODERATELY DIFFICULT PUZZLES

Complete these "Wheel of Fortune"-type puzzles, using the clue on the left.

1. phrase   _ e _ w _ x _   _ _ d
   _ e _ w _ _ n
2. things   _ n _ _ _ l   _ r _ _ k _ _ s
3. people   _ _ s _ _ _ r s   _ r _ m
   _ u _ _ r   s p _ _ _
4. phrase   _ s   _ t   _ o _   _ n   h _ r _
   _ r   _ s   _ t   j _ _ t   _ e?
5. person   _ _ _ n   R _ _ e _ _
6. thing   _ e l l _   _ _ l l _ _ s
7. thing   _ o _ t _ m _   _ e w _ _ _ y
8. people   _ i e _ e _ s
9. person   _ e _ _ _   _ a v _ _
10. thing   p _ _ i m _ _ y

Answers: 1. betwixt and between **2.** animal crackers **3.** visitors from outer space **4.** Is it hot in here or is it just me? **5.** Joan Rivers **6.** jelly bellies **7.** costume jewelry **8.** dieters **9.** Bette Davis **10.** palimony

HARD PUZZLES

Complete these puzzles from "Scrabble"-like puzzles using the clue on the left.

1. A small body of water _ e _ r _ _ o _
2. They take their place in history _ _ u _ e _ _ s
3. Some of them are high rollers _ _ v _ s
4. Some of them are six feet under _ r _ _ t
5. A real bird brain _ _ _ _ t y
6. Some of them are spicy _ _ o _ _ e s
7. One for the road _ a _ d _ r _ _
8. Jack climbed through them _ l _ _ d s

Answers: 1. teardrop **2.** students **3.** waves **4.** trout **5.** tweety **6.** stories **7.** wanderer **8.** clouds

EASY GENERAL-KNOWLEDGE QUESTIONS

These questions are similar to those used on "Sale of the Century."

1. What country's currency is based on the "deutsche mark"? ____________
2. The second sign of the zodiac takes its name from the Latin word for "bull." Name it. ____________
3. Name the hero who was immortalized in a poem that begins, "Listen my children and you shall hear. . . ."
____
4. Big hits by this pop balladeer include "Mandy" and "I Write the Songs." Name him. ____________

5. What suave fictional hero made his film debut in the 1962 hit *Dr. No*? ________________
6. When Richard Nixon resigned the presidency in 1974, who replaced him as chief executive? ________

Answers: 1. Germany **2.** Taurus **3.** Paul Revere **4.** Barry Manilow **5.** James Bond **6.** Gerald Ford

MODERATELY DIFFICULT GENERAL-KNOWLEDGE QUESTIONS

These questions are like those used on "Hollywood Squares," "Sale of the Century," and "Jeopardy!"

1. It's Italy's most popular spectator sport. ________
2. In the 1978 *TV Guide* poll, he was voted best-liked and least-liked sportscaster. ________________
3. British versions of these U.S. game shows were "Celebrity Squares," "Family Fortunes," and "Criss Cross Squares." ________________
4. For "Here You Come Again," she became the first country artist to receive a platinum record. ________

   ____
5. According to Ann Landers, the three things that hold a marriage together are love, respect, and what? ____
6. On TV, where did you see sweat hogs? ________
7. True or false: most male gorillas are only interested in getting romantically involved about once a year. ___
8. Gandhi, the great Indian leader was called *Mahatma* by his people. What does *Mahatma* mean? ______
9. According to superstition, the seventh son of the sev-

enth son will have a very special gift. What is that gift? ______

10. What "a" word does *Playboy* magazine say has the best nightlife of any U.S. ski area? ______

Answers: 1. soccer **2.** Howard Cosell **3.** "Hollywood Squares," "Family Feud," and "Tic Tac Dough" **4.** Dolly Parton **5.** loyalty **6.** "Welcome Back, Kotter" **7.** true **8.** great soul **9.** healing powers **10.** Aspen

HARD GENERAL-KNOWLEDGE QUESTIONS

These questions are similar to those used on "Jeopardy!"

1. Who was our very first secretary of state in 1789? Was it Alexander Hamilton, Thomas Jefferson, or Benjamin Franklin? ______

2. Some say that this author's first novel, *The Naked and the Dead*, is the best novel to emerge from World War II. ______

3. Of Ohio, Indiana, and Illinois, the state most densely populated and having the most large cities is ______

4. In biology, what two-word term do we use for an animal whose body temperature varies with that of its environment? ______

5. A bird, an exit, or a boring story—what is an egress? ______

6. What French word describes military troops trained to serve on horseback? ______

7. In mythology, what chubby cherub was the Roman god of love? ______

8. What last name is shared by father and daughter actors Efrem and Stephanie? ______

9. Who are the most notoriously famous families of Logan County, Virginia, and Pike County, Kentucky? ______________________

10. What singer-turned-actress appeared in such films as *Mask* and *Silkwood*? ______________________

Answers: 1. Thomas Jefferson **2.** Norman Mailer **3.** Ohio **4.** cold-blooded **5.** exit **6.** cavalry **7.** Eros **8.** Zimbalist **9.** the Hatfields and McCoys **10.** Cher

LOGIC AND LUCK QUESTIONS

These questions are from "Card Sharks." Keep in mind that in the real game your opponent would have the chance to win by guessing whether your answer is "higher" or "lower" than the actual number.

1. Before the show, we asked *ten bachelors* in our studio audience "Have you ever stolen a girl away from another man?" How many of those ten bachelors said they had stolen a girl away from another man? ______
2. We surveyed one hundred *married women* and we asked them, "Do you think you would be able to support your family as well as your husband does?" How many married women said they would be able to support their family as well as their husbands? ______________
3. *Educated Guess:* What is the fastest speed that an American spacecraft has ever gone? (Please give your answer in thousands of miles per hour.) ____________
4. We surveyed one hundred *married men* and asked them, "When your wife has a cold, do you refuse to kiss

her?'' How many married men said they do refuse to kiss their wives? ____________________

5. We surveyed one hundred *Catholic priests* and asked them, ''If church laws were changed to allow priests to marry, would you get married?'' How many priests said they would get married? ____________________

Answers: 1. 6 **2.** 36 **3.** 3(8,000) **4.** 16 **5.** 25

Guess the cost of each item. These questions are similar to those used on ''The Price Is Right.''

1. What is the price of a new Italian surrey (carriage)—$2,245 or $2,792? ____________________
2. A camping trailer is marked $4,5095. There is one number too many. Which one should be taken out? ____________________
3. You can win a new Chevrolet Spectrum and car stereo by guessing its price. You guess the price by first seeing a numbered and signed lithograph worth $825. Is the first digit of the price of the car an 8 or 2 or 5? Next is a recliner worth $600. Is the 6 or 0 the next digit? $383 cash is next. Is a 3 or 8 the next digit? A curio cabinet worth $300. A 3 or 0? You may change any one digit in the car's price if you think it's incorrect. You now have a choice of stopping the game and keeping all the prizes listed above or you can risk them all and try to guess the actual price of the car. Remember every digit has to be correct for you to win. ____________________

Answers: 1. $2,245 **2.** 0 **3.** $8,630

These questions are from "The Newlywed Game." Answer them with your spouse and see how well you know each other.

1. Husbands, which old TV show does your wife's family remind you of: "The Munsters," "The Monkees," or "The Mickey Mouse Club?" ____________
2. Does your wife think you've had more trouble making: money, whoopee, sense, or making her happy? ____
3. My wife hates to play peekaboo with me because when I peek at her *blank*, I like to yell "boo!" ________
4. Wives, what was the last thing at home that you did that made him roar with laughter but wasn't funny to you? ____________________
5. I really think my husband is long overdue for a good (blank) ____________________
6. What type of fruit does your husband's chest remind you of? ____________________

These questions are from "The Dating Game."

(*Bachelor to bachelorettes*)

1. If I came to you and told you I hurt my little finger, what would you do? ______________
2. What's the best part of bachelorette number 3? ____

   ____
3. If I was Tarzan and you were Jane, tell me why I should swing with you. ____________

(*Bachelorette to bachelors*)

4. What do you and I have in common that the rest of the bachelors don't? ______________
5. How would you amuse me on a rainy day? ________

   ____
6. Sing me a song about why you want me to pick you for my date. ____________________